D0062878

THE BATTLE FOR THE AMERICAN CHURCH
REVISITED

Msgr. George A. Kelly

The Battle for the American Church Revisited

IGNATIUS PRESS   SAN FRANCISCO

Cover by Roxanne Mei Lum

CONTENTS

5

INTRODUCTION

Fifteen years ago, Doubleday and Company published a book to which its editors assigned the title *The Battle for the American Church*. Paul VI had died a short time before, and the pontificate of John Paul II had only just begun. The opening paragraph of that book read:

> A guerilla-type warfare is going on inside the Church and its outcome is clearly doubtful. The Pope and Roman Curia are fending off with mixed success the attacks of their own theologians who, in the name of scholarship, demand more radical accommodation with Protestant and secular thought. The issues at stake are the correctness of Catholic doctrine and the survival of the Catholic Church as a significant influence in the life of her own communicants.

The word "radical" was used purposely. The essence of Protestantism is "private judgment", that of secularism, "this world". In New Testament times, the "freedom of the Sons of God" and the solicitous care of the human condition, first of all by deacons, were important Christian principles; but judgments or priorities opposed to the common faith or to God's Word were always censurable by the Catholic Church's authority. The real issue at that time was not the power of the ecclesiastical hierarchy to rule but the authority of Christ: to teach all of God's Word and have his Truth guaranteed by the pope and those bishops in union with him.

The book and its thesis received modest attention, sometimes favorable, just as often angry. One Washington journalist, a former religious, was entranced by the book but wondered in print, "Doesn't the author know that 'The Battle' is over?" That was 1979. Today, however, as the pontificate of John Paul II begins to wind down, the time may be opportune to ask: Who did win the battle? Or is it still going on? And, if so, when will it end? And with what results for those who fully believe that the Catholic Church is the Church of Christ and that he was the Son of God? The commentary to follow is another effort by the original writer to answer the questions he raised back then.

This manuscript has been reviewed, in whole or in part, by twelve members of Catholic academe, by two pastors, and by two bishops, to whom the author is grateful, although obviously he alone is responsible for its contents. Special appreciation is due also to William and Bernadette Kimmig for the production, reproduction, and editing of many drafts.

Chapter One

Revisiting the Battle

When Doubleday's John Delaney asked this writer in 1978 whether he could assemble suitable material to deal with what was then being called "the uncertain Church", a *Commonweal* staff writer, assisting Delaney at the time, reading the text, labeled it "The Battle for the American Church". The name stuck, and a year later a book was published with this title.

Almost simultaneously, Cardinal Aegidio Vagnozzi came to New York, to await the newly elected John Paul II who was en route to Boston. One day, walking a Rockaway boardwalk, he announced that Jean Jadot, one of his successors as apostolic delegate, was being recalled by Rome. Vagnozzi expressed annoyance that the decision, apparently made a year earlier, had not thus far been implemented. He seemed pleased to add that Pio Laghi was being brought in from Argentina and would be given five years "to clean up the American Church". Archbishop Laghi arrived in due course (1980) and soon assured me that every one of his staff was reading *The Battle* at his instruction. He did not know the Vagnozzi tale then, but in 1985 I related it to him, asking him with a smile, "Have you cleaned it up?" To which Laghi responded, in equally good humor: "They just gave me five more years."

However much he evaded the question with that jest, Laghi initially worried about the implications of the phrase "American Church". He was not alone. John Delaney had simply thought this phrase more mellifluous than "Church in the United States".

Neither John Delaney nor I, God forbid, had had any intention of our Church being anything less than fully Roman Catholic.

Many scholarly and other journal articles, before and since, have been written about the travail of the Catholic Church after the completion of the Second Vatican Council. The writers of these articles fall into two categories—those who consider the aftermath to have been something of a sellout of Catholic substance, and those who wrote, and write, as if the revolutionary *fait accompli* following 1965 was just what Christ had in mind. An antidote, perhaps, to the Catholic distortions created by post-evangelicals or civil rulers and still foisted on people by the hierarchy. *The Battle,* while less unsympathetic to the critics of radical upheaval than to the revolutionaries, was more a report of the latter's clearly stated agenda, already at work, some of which the Church authority in the United States (not Rome at the time) had begun to adopt as its own. In those days of postconciliar enthusiasm, little calculus was made of what this agenda would do to the faith and practice of those who went to Church every Sunday, or to their children, who were attached to the Church only by the rite of Baptism. One bishop, after reading *The Battle,* accused me of being unfriendly to him. To which I responded: "No, I merely quoted what you said in public." The prelate obviously was embarrassed by the reminder that he was one of those officeholders who had failed to take the revolutionaries at their word.

Fr. Louis Bouyer, the French liturgist responsible for much of what went into the Council's 1965 document on the liturgy, was so disgusted by the post–Vatican II situation that he wrote *The Decomposition of Catholicism* only two years later. That same year, the American philosopher Deitrich von Hildebrand wrote his *Trojan Horse within the Church,* a book which, when reissued as a reputed "classic" in 1993, was praised by John Cardinal O'Connor for its prophetic insights. Subsequent works which favored the upheavals within the Catholic community, or which claimed to represent the authentic reforms of the Council, included ex-priest Peter Hebblethwaite's *The Runaway Church* (1975), ex-priest Jay P. Dolan's *The American Catholic Experience* (1985), and one-time USCC employee Jim Castelli's *The American Catholic People* (with George Gallup) and *The Emerging Parish* (with Msgr. Joseph Gremillion), both in 1987. In 1994, Jesuit James Schall asked a more searching question: *Does Catholicism Still Exist?*

Who can deny that many recent accommodations to Protestant and secular forces have been "radical"? Not, of course, in the propositions which define Catholic doctrine and moral norms, but in the institutional arrangements developed over centuries to teach God's revealed Word and worship correctly. The documents of reform and renewal from Rome have never been more numerous or profound, but they do little to regulate latter-day Catholic institutions or Catholic lives at the street level.

Whether pastors are situated at the top or center of the Catholic community, the fact is that the contemporary Church is being run today often from the sidelines. The Pope is well aware that local Catholic communities are watering down or stonewalling Roman definitions and decrees; that local bishops are more dominated by their national body than their predecessors ever were and are more likely to bow to their presbyterates than to enforce canon or liturgical law strictly; that pastors defer to what were once called curates; that priests are often intimidated enough by religious or laity to avoid doing the right thing, lest in controversy they find themselves alone, unsupported by the diocese. Pious Catholics, facing scandalous conduct in their parish, no longer can be sure of a responsive hearing unless they threaten trouble, which good Catholics rarely do. Many bishops still have a sense of who they are—like the one who, observing a pastor substituting his own Eucharistic Prayers in the Mass, privately warned the offender: "If you, or any other priest, do that again, I'll wipe Main Street with your body!" Or the bishop who, presiding at a nonliturgical dance by a veritable Salome during a Sunday liturgy, whispered to the pastor on his right: "If she asks for a head, she'll get yours!" More than a few bishops or pastors simply throw up their hands with a plea for understanding: "What can I do?" Or, "I can't mandate that." The Church may be a sacramental Church, but it is not uncommon to hear laity complain, when they object to something they know is wrong—like postponed First Confession or inept First Communion rituals—that they often receive this disclaimer from the priest: "Oh, I have nothing to do with that. You'll have to take it up with the nuns."

There is presently a cultural mood in secular society which, in the name of privacy and freedom, sanctions many behavior patterns that disrupt social order and disedify the young. Church authority, too, has been reluctant to use restraining force on those who undermine the peace and doctrine of the Catholic community. A one-time *New York Times* religion editor, also a Protestant minister, has written a new book, *Holy Siege: The Year That Shook Catholic America* (1993), purportedly analyzing the alleged crackdown on American Catholics in 1987 by John Paul II. There was no real "crackdown", to be sure. But the implication of the 594-page volume is that popes rightfully have no such governing authority. As if to reinforce this point, the *Times* itself solicited a favorable review of the book from an ex-priest who once did writing for the National Conference of Catholic Bishops.

Many months ago I and a friend, an internationally known theologian, mused over this aspect of the contemporary Church problem. He took the view that the situation called for good teachers in the episcopacy; my sense was that "good governance" was the greater need. The differing emphases were not mutually exclusive, simply different. Once upon a time two bishops worked side by side, one a first-rate preacher but a less than competent administrator, the other a good administrator who said very little unless it was written out for him. The latter left behind him a flowering diocese whose majority of churchgoers (and supporters) were Italian-Americans. He had succeeded in doing what none of his predecessors had done—cajoling, flattering, and pressuring Italian pastors to build parochial schools—while at the same time he himself was expanding his high-school system to deepen the Catholic formation of families whose fathers rarely went to Mass. Considering that Italian-Americans today are the backbone of that diocese's churchgoing public, it is clear that the nonverbal bishop was in fact the better teacher.

A house well run is a better school than one with a martinet father or a nagging mother. A house well run has purpose, warmth, expected rules of conduct, rewards for good behavior, punishments for disorder and disobedience, and is administered by parents who love their children and are competent in their role. The Catholic Church has not had that kind of governance since the death of Pius XII.

The Surprising Beginnings of Trouble

Pius XII had a sixth sense that troubles were brewing for the Church in Europe. His *Humanae generis* in 1950 telegraphed those anxieties about undisciplined thinkers emerging within the Church. There he found fifty-six doctrinal errors against the faith circulating through the corridors of Catholic universities and seminaries. The denial of original sin was only one of these, although the existence of original sin is a doctrine which underpins the Christian worldview of Christ's importance to the world. The year before he died (1957), he went after European Jesuits for bootlegging heterodox opinions into Catholic institutions, driving them farther underground for at least five more years. On the American front, things were comparatively peaceful, since the Church here was bursting at the seams with faithful Catholics. Many of the best Catholics were the graduates of Catholic higher education, made so in part by their professors. There were stirrings, to be sure, over Church-and-state issues and about how many children

Catholic parents should have to fulfill the command to "increase and multiply". The accusation that Catholics were not very intellectual (by secular standards, that is), introduced by a Catholic university professor, was not taken seriously, except in small elite circles for whom a Nobel Prize was more to be valued than a comparable papal medal. Still, by Council time, the mood of American academics verged on the discontent of their vocal European counterparts, such as Bernard Häring. When Apostolic Delegate Vagnozzi gave a warning at Marquette University (1961) to adventuresome theologians here similar to that given by Pope Pius, the roars of indignation were heard from the Catholic University of America to Notre Dame.

Pius XII seemed to sense the desirability of holding an ecumenical council to deal with growing missionary and catechetical problems, but he used advanced age as an excuse for avoiding such a convocation. Yet, he was also more judicious than his successor and preferred to reform according to design and with built-in safeguards. In addition to his liturgical innovations and the creation of the International Federation of Catholic Universities in 1949 and the Conference of Major Superiors following the 1952 world meeting in Rome were forward-looking moves. These reforms were well received in the United States and contributed to the improved quality of our educational structures. These creations became runaway infrastructures after the Council.

Pius XII, like Pius XI before him and John XXIII later, looked upon the American Church of that day as a model for the exhausted ecclesial bodies of Continental Europe. No modern democratic society anywhere enjoyed at that time as vital and believing a Catholic presence as did the United States of America. Critics would be hard-pressed to find its equal anywhere, either in its institutions or in its pious masses.

Many of the leading priests and laity of my generation—at the parish or diocesan level—were by World War II in the vanguard of those social, ecumenical, and liturgical movements which became the identifying marks of the "new" authentic Catholicity which typified the Vatican II era. John A. Ryan, Dorothy Day, Virgil Michel, John Courtney Murray, Alexander Schneider, Reynold Hillenbrand, Herbert Ratner, John La Farge, Andrée Emery, and John Patrick Monaghan were ahead of their bishops, perhaps, but they were also fully believing and obedient Catholics. Their voices might have reflected aspects of Catholicity often unappreciated in chancery offices of the 1950s or at the street levels of the Church. Yet, what the "streets" might have considered "radical" at the time was authentic Catholic teaching, validated time and time again by the highest authorities of the Church. If, as events proved, the seeming innovators were leading their hierarchy in matters of special competence, they never pretended, even by indirection, that their role among the clergy or the faithful was to upstage, contradict, or rival Church authority. However critical of Church governance any one of them might have been in particular circumstances, they were protagonists, not antagonists. And, if Church hierarchy did not always appreciate the "nuances" or the public posturing of these specialists, the same authority would rarely hesitate to disapprove or reject, particularly within Catholic institutions, any conduct, even that involving prudential judgments, which disrupted the worship or piety of the Catholic people or the Church's integrity before the opinion-molders of the country. The style of episcopal leadership within the vast regions of continental America varied, as did the particular causes agitating enlightened elites. Nonetheless, elites together with their bishops were solidly committed to the promotion and defense of "one Lord, one Faith, one Baptism". Even *Commonweal* still adhered to "the presentation of orthodox religious principles" proclaimed in its founding editorial (November 12, 1924). In those early years, hierarchy might haggle over where to place the Catholic university, whether to condemn the Knights of Labor or a proposed child labor law. But when the issue was a Baltimore Catechism, opposed by some intellectuals, or a national Catholic school system, opposed by Americanists, or when it involved the doctrine on marriage contained in *Casti connubii,* rejected by some European prelates, American bishops moved daringly in unison, as if to say "Damn the opposition, full speed ahead!" They gained thereby the major credit (in the words of Bishop Gerald Shaughnessy in 1925) for "building the Church in the United States better than they knew".

The Second Vatican Council, while changing nothing in traditional claims or doctrines, did shift ecclesial priorities and did create a new mood among bishops to accommodate what Catholicity is, or ought to be, to the insistent claims of modern academics. The conciliar debates initiated by John XXIII during the 1960s left an impression that a Church compromise with hitherto-rejected scholarly nuances of Christianity was possible. The electronic and other media of the period complicated the Church's noble effort by simplifying intricate doctrinal issues foreign to the modern mind and by giving more positive coverage to critics of Church policies than to spokesmen for tradition. The 1960s was a decade of revolution for which the hierarchy, beginning with the Pope, were ill prepared. Moreover, Vatican II was not intended, as practically all earlier councils had been, to cure particular heresies or schisms; in theory, it functioned merely to update structures and to reorder programs. To meet the demands of modernity for a more enjoyable and freer life on earth, not merely to pursue the life to come—these accommodations by the Church were "a sign of the times", or so it was said.

However, serious biblical, moral, catechetical, pastoral, and institutional devices, with an explosive potential, were also planted all over the Church during the Council. By demythologizing the Word of God as taught by the Church (via historical criticism), by relativizing moral norms (via proportionalism), by making personal experience of religion (not its content) the preferred teaching tool, by preferring conscientious discovery and willing collaboration to assent and obedience, by stressing compassion over judgment, reconciliation over penance, positive proclamations over negative commandments, the Church made it possible for "change makers" to raise questions about which Catholic definitions and moral norms might not be so unchangeable, after all. As a result, to those who had hitherto looked to the Church with assurance that what she taught was true, hierarchical authority, even if Christ were its source, seemed enervated.

Richard John Neuhaus, a convert priest, once described the perils that befell mainline Protestantism, whose churches today, from week to week, are relatively empty, save at concert time or on a spectacular occasion. About the time that its leadership learned from scholars that its dogmatic claims were unverifiable, Christianity's social mission became the priority, not the creeds. The recent attack by German theologians on John Paul II's *Veritatis splendor*, an attack calling upon the Pope to defend humanist causes instead of conducting a crusade on behalf of revealed moral absolutes, is of a similar genre. Doctrinal divisiveness between professors and pastors had plagued German Lutheranism during Bismarck's time. The same loss of clear purpose began to characterize the contemporary American Catholic Church shortly after the Council. In the Catholic case, the downturns were quite unnecessary. The Church's social mission and her humanist aspirations or successes are irrelevant if her dogmatic claims are dubious or untrue. The human race does not need a Church to complement the state as an instrument of human betterment in this world. The Catholic Church herself disclaims any competence in sociopolitical affairs, save for providing moral guidance. Indeed, she justifies herself primarily as the instrument of God, leading mankind to its eternal destiny, a function that requires the Church to seek first God's kingdom. To support the human aspirations of her believers and potential converts (even of her enemies), those who live in this world or are victimized by it, is a coordinate but a subsidiary ecclesial role. Pope St. Gregory the Great had the Catholic scale about right: "If you cannot give up everything of this world, at least keep what belongs to the world in such a way that you yourself are not kept prisoners of the world" (PL 76, 1272).

After Vatican II, leading Catholics failed to exercise such discretion, accepting the rhetoric of internal humanistic critics: that the Church was too otherworldly, too authoritative, too hierarchical, too detached from the oppression, poverty, and suffering in the world. "Freedom", especially, became a clarion call for change without anyone having defined its religious meaning. One humorous incident, which symbolized the erratic nature of the times, occurred in New York. At the Council's end, Cardinal Spellman invited Cardinal Leo Suenens of Belgium to address his Sisters of Charity. Suenens, who exercised tight control over religious women in his own archdiocese (Malines), that day preached a full-blown message of freedom for religious. On the way home, through the curved roads of Mount St. Vincent's College, Spellman's car was forced into a ditch by a little Volkswagen, which careened around a corner, depositing Suenens on the floor. When the Belgian rose to ask, "What was that?" the New York Cardinal puckishly replied: "Those were two of your liberated nuns." To which the Belgian replied: "They're going too far!" Spellman loved to tell that story. And Suenens, later in life, had reason to regret the liberation message he had given to Paul VI during the Council, a message which brought belated papal disfavor, once the dysfunctions of Suenen's influence became apparent to the Pope.

Therefore, a case can be made that the Council's thrust, if it was intended to improve the Church's evangelical position on the eve of her second millennium, failed in this objective. Far from engaging modernity constructively, the Church almost immediately adopted some of its worst features, compromising her own dignity and the sanctity of her persons, places, and programs. Her political role in secular society was also weakened once her hold on the consciences of her people was attenuated. Convoking a universal assembly of bishops without fully calculating the wide range of difficulties that might ensue turned out to be a strategic blunder. Paul VI later said that three years in addition to the three allotted were needed for such a Council, but the die had been cast. The debates themselves tended to make the Church seem ambiguous about her long-held doctrine that sexuality and marriage were primarily about family and children, thus opening the door to the sexual revolution. The hasty decentralization of ecclesial machinery into national conferences of Catholic bishops, which occurred without proper safeguards, was another improvident concession to modernity. It gave legitimacy to anti-Church activity by disgruntled elites and their populist supporters. Within those early Council and postconciliar years, a rash of antiestablishment Catholic books took a prominent place in the forefront of activism on behalf of a new Church, and most of them became required reading in seminars for teachers, in seminary classes, in monasteries and convents, tending in one way or another to belittle the Catholic faith which most of their readership had come to know, love, and live.[1]

And, as if the debunking scholarship were not sufficient to damage the Church of the sixties, there was more of the same done at the street level whenever the Church was called "a whore" (Phillip Berrigan); when a bishop was described as a "drunken father [whom] we tried to hide when company comes, and we worry about what half-wit blunders he will make next" (John

[1] Raymond E. Brown, *Priest and Bishop* (Paulist Press, 1970); James A. Coriden, *The Case for Freedom* (Corpus, 1969); Charles Curran, *Dissent in and for the Church* (Sheed and Ward, 1969); Avery Dulles, *Models of the Church* (Doubleday, 1974); Bernard Häring, *Christian Renewal in a Changing World* (Desclee, 1964); Robert Blair Kaiser, *Pope, Council and World* (Macmillan, 1965); Eugene C. Kennedy, *The People Are the Church* (Doubleday, 1969); Hans Küng, *The Council in Action* (Sheed and Ward, 1963); Xavier Rynne, *Letters from Vatican City* (Farrer, Strauss, 1963, 1965, 1966); George Tavard, *The Pilgrim Church* (Herder, 1967); Edward Wakim and Joseph F. Scheuer, *The De-Romanization of the American Catholic Church* (Macmillan, 1966). Of particular significance were the Brown and Dulles books, one suggesting that Christ might not have had a separate church in mind, the other indicating that an institutional church was not viable in a post–Vatican II world.

McKenzie, S.J.); when religious orders were doomed "as already dead" (Gabriel Moran); when the laity was seen as products of "the dogma factory centered in Rome" (Gary Wills). Such snide treatment of the institutional Church, of the priesthood, and of the sacred reinforced what more sophisticated academics were saying in their classroom settings. Partly to be agreeable, partly to keep peace, bishops accepted their more dangerous critics into their own households.

Reviewing this situation from the hindsight of today makes argument easy for those who, from the beginning, correctly judged that the Council did not change Church doctrine. Policies, priorities, methodologies, *yes*; but doctrine and morals, *no*. All one has to do is read the Catechism of the Catholic Church or John Paul II's *Veritatis splendor* on moral theology, both of current vintage, to know how right the denigrated "conservatives" were. Take the contraception issue. When Rome surveyed bishops all over the world on that subject in 1964, 167 of the 168 American bishop respondents affirmed the teaching of *Casti connubii*. (Cardinal Cicognani, then the secretary of state to Paul VI, rued that one negative reply: "I made him!") But by 1965 the expectation of radical change had grown intense at high levels. Cardinal Cicognani was already talking encyclical, but within the new NCWC, Washington staff house guests could stay up until the wee hours of the morning trying to persuade important episcopal advisors, unsuccessfully, that the Church doctrine on contraception would not be changed. Sniping in the NCWC at the valiant efforts of Jesuit John Ford to save the Birth Control Commission from itself was not uncommon, and the equally devoted son of the Church, Msgr. John C. Knott, NCWC's family life director, was often a lonely figure, along with Bishop Paul Tanner, NCWC's general secretary. But the mood for change in the bishops' own headquarters was in place, even before the Council's end.

What Has Been Going On

At first, "the Battle" for the Catholic soul seemed to be an in-house argument over how to make an old faith better understood. Generations of Americans, even if Catholic, indoctrinated by secular educators and opinion-molders to accept nothing on faith, or very little "from authority", needed better explanations of religion, it was said. But once theoretical reformulations got underway, seriously in academe and seemingly everywhere later on, the Church suffered heavy losses. Indeed, the decrease in Catholic numbers since 1962 is startling for a Church once heralded as a jewel in Rome's ecclesiastical tiara. Many latter-day commentators, often priests, dismiss claims of a "golden Church era", asserting that less obvious Catholics are the price we must pay for exchanging the ghetto for modern maturity.[2] Folklore of another kind placed major responsibility for the Church's present malaise mainly on secular forces unleashed by Einstein's theory of relativity or on the discovery of the birth-control pill. Or on the civil-rights' movement's consciousness raising. Or on space-age technology, such as electronic media, which mass-produced secular values exclusively. Maybe so. But, by virtue of her long experience, the Church might have been expected to deal more efficaciously with a sudden upheaval. As a revealed religion with specific credal truths, guaranteed by successors to the apostles, and as a voluntary association to which members and their clergy were committed only by professed personal faith, the Catholic Church had long since developed secure defenses against invasions by Protestantism or secularism.

Surprisingly, however, the dysfunctions following the Second Vatican Council began almost immediately in the United States:

— The Church, whose fundamental function is the worship of God in the Eucharist, suffered a severe decrease in Sunday

[2] See Walter O'Malley, S.J., *The Critic,* Fall 1993, p. 98.

Mass attendance, from the highest rate in the non-Catholic world to levels more in common with the less-practicing populations in Europe.

—The Church, which once averaged three priests for each of her eighteen thousand parishes, most of them young to middle-age and American born, suffered flight from the priesthood and religious life to an alarming extent.

—Many dioceses began to be financially strapped; some verged on bankruptcy.

—The largest Catholic school system in the world fell into rapid decline, feeding a growing suspicion that (at the elementary and high-school levels) it will be virtually extinct sometime in the twenty-first century.

—Those who can afford to pay high tuition rates, or who are subsidized, will still enter Catholic schools, but the purpose for which these schools were created a century ago will have been vitiated.

—The only form of education still bearing the name Catholic that is now growing numerically is the college system, but for all practical purposes it now places higher value on its secular service than on its religious reason for existence.

—The results of a remarkable array of opinion studies indicate that (a) Catholic youth are so badly trained under Catholic auspices that they are called "religious illiterates"; and (b) their parents, although the majority are still churchgoers, now think like non-Catholics and are often praised in enlightened circles for a "pick and choose" Catholicity.

—The Catholic hierarchy, presiding officers in a sacramental Church, encounter problems today never faced by their predecessors, at least in this century: high rates of premarital copulation, lower rates of valid marriage and infant births, increased divorces on a par with other Americans, widespread use of contraception and/or sterilization, even among churchgoers, general acceptance of abortion in special circumstances, a high enough rate of diocesan-approved annulments to create the impression that marriage for Catholics is no longer necessarily indissoluble. (Sixty thousand annulments annually, 80 percent of the Church's world total, do not offer evidence at the parish level of Vatican II's call for holiness as the chief mark of ecclesial reform.)

— The Church which, following Christ, taught that deadly sin is the most serious obex to her people's happiness here, and to salvation hereafter, and must be submitted by Christ's will to a penitential process, has within a quarter-century experienced the virtual disappearance of the sacrament of Penance. Furthermore, Church leaders seem unable to reinstitute its common use.

— The most sacred of all sacraments, the Eucharist, repository of Christ's living Body, whose reception was intended by him to be the Church's simplest indication of personal and ecclesial holiness, is now widely received by many who are living in serious sin. Certain theologians, and a few bishops, ignore this practice of unworthy reception, condemned today by John Paul II as it was by St. Paul in the beginning.

Polling results or guesswork based on samples do not a scientific study make about a living body. Growth and decline have their providential aspects. The Catholic Directory annually publishes increases in the Church population, but these guesses hardly reflect growth in ecclesial piety. And that is the question of importance. About twenty years ago, the cover of Newsweek asked: Has the Catholic Church Lost Its Soul? Even though the question was posed by a Catholic editor, who years earlier had lost confidence in the truths of the Church he did not like, the answer is more uncertain today than it was then. Bishops point to the crowds in their cathedrals or to assemblies in Denver when the charismatic John Paul II arrives as signs of continued vitality. That there is ongoing spiritual life in our Church no one can doubt. That the Catholic liturgy, well done, is a great religious event is also beyond dispute. That the evidence of residual piety is there for all to see on Ash Wednesday, at retreats, and at novenas, and surely at weekly Masses during Advent and Lent, wherever Catholics fifty-five years and older gather, need not even be argued. That few other institutions in the United States, not even free-spending government, do more for the poor on the streets than the Catholic Church is a marvel of ours, or any other, time. Still, the Catholic Church is living off the patrimony of those immigrants of old and their children, who built our cathedrals, our hospitals, our schools, and our convents.

Ask practicing grandparents today about their adult children, who demonstrate little interest in the Church or what she teaches even though their parents gave them a full Catholic education at the sacrifice of a new car or a vacation; ask them about the continued presence in major Church institutions, including seminaries, of priests and/or religious who no longer believe fully what the Church teaches *magisterially;* or about those explanations of sexual aberrations among the clergy which blame stunted psychological growth rather than the breakdown of the Church's moral discipline; or about official silence of authorities in the face of arrogant behavior by religious, often women, who, in spite of the evangelical counsels to which they are vowed, frequently live lives inconsistent with their ecclesial commitment; ask about clergy and religious who use their Catholic position to pursue a political agenda to the neglect of piety.

Older parish priests have the opportunity late in life to chat with their once young parishioners, now nearing Social Security status. When those who blessed themselves as they passed a church, the ones who attended weekday Mass during Lent or confessed at least monthly, speak aloud these days, they speak lovingly of the Church of their youth. They also remark how wide and deep are the differences between the post–World War II Church and post–Vatican II Church. American clerics of that period recall how entranced they were at the time with the mystique of the French Church: a Georges Bernanos and his country abbé, an Étienne Gilson and his revelation-based philosophy, a Cardinal Suhard and his world-famous pastorals. For many parish priests, Abbé Michonneau's *Revolution in the City Parish* was a bible.

We did not realize how vibrant American parochial life was until we read Michonneau. His entire apostolate (like Canon Cardijn's) called for the revitalization of Christianity in "Catholic" France, which he considered absolutely pagan. Low Mass attendance, alienated working classes, parishes sustained by old ladies, ritual Catholicity without internalized faith. And, from First Communion till Extreme Unction, most French Catholics, in his judgment, had mind-sets like those who had no religious faith at all. During the 1950s, American curates readily found out they had nothing much to learn from Michonneau, or even from Suhard. Our bishops of that day may not have been as brilliant as the Archbishop in Paris. Indeed, they were hardly ever mentioned on the streets where we lived. Nor were American pastors known for writing books. Yet, our parish predecessors had bequeathed to us so many believing and practicing Catholics that, by Michonneau's standards, they could never be identified as pagan.

In 1994, on the other hand, American grandparents might well often agree that Michonneau's view of paganized Catholics is verified in the lives of their grandchildren. In the lives of some of their children, too. And in aging peers, who have joined the chorus of those who now believe that the Church of their youth, by making them feel guilty about committing sin, deprived them of full maturity as human beings.

Chapter Two

What the Battle Is All About

Do we let the breakdown run its course? Or do Church authorities take steps to recapture her well-known unity of purpose and role?

Almost thirty years ago, the mayor of New York City asked the archbishop of New York to assemble the pastors of New York for a discussion of city problems. As the meeting progressed, it was clear that the city fathers wanted the Church fathers to do what they could to keep the Italian and Italian-American families within county borders. They were the last stable population group left from those days when New Yorkers could walk the streets at night without fear of being mugged. As the afternoon was coming to its end, an Italian pastor of significance, and a very funny fellow with an accent that had changed little since his walk down the gangplank a generation earlier, took possession of the microphone to say: "Mr. Mayor, I'm the pastor of a multi-ethnic family parish whose parishioners remain in New York because of their Church, particularly because of its school system. They'll stay for a while. But we cannot hope to keep them for long, because the City of New York has given over control of its streets to sociopaths. Until you can tell me what you are doing to regain control of the streets, so that my people can once again walk them safely, I cannot tell you how long these people will stay." That Italian pastor was right. Today his neighborhood is drug-filled and crime-racked, and the Italian families are all but gone.

Something of this kind has happened to the Church. The

Scriptures may say that "it is required of stewards that they be found trustworthy" (1 Cor 4:2), but the dissenters and the disobedient have taken control of major Church streets, without considering themselves in the least unfaithful. Discipleship customarily means discipline, but that is often called repression by those who wish to live within the Church only according to their own norms and rules.

Observers of the Catholic scene legitimately ask: How can this happen to a Church so well versed in the evil doings of God's creatures? Is it not the Church's function to reform evil lives? For pastors to protect the flock? Years ago, Karl Menninger opined that the one Christian doctrine with abundant empirical evidence to substantiate its truth was "original sin". The Church's role becomes more difficult when, in her classrooms, academics consign this truth to the netherworld of biblical mythology. Established to see that her members do good, the Church owes her existence to a gentle Redeemer who preached the reward of heaven for the faithful and "everlasting darkness" for the irrevocably unfaithful; earthly punishment, too, for those who in this life scandalize his "little ones". In New Testament times, the first apostles quarantined recalcitrant members who seriously disturbed the faith and morals of the Christian community. St. Paul reminded his disciple Timothy that evildoers needed careful scrutiny. In the First Letter to him (5:20), Timothy was instructed: "The ones who do commit sins are to be publicly reprimanded, so that the rest may fear to offend." Throughout history many have disputed St. Paul, but the question he raised still needs a Christian answer: Is a given individual's freedom within the Church a higher value than the Church's common good?

No one denies the tension built into the relationship of individuals with all societies, including the Church. Just prior to Martin Luther's revolution, the rather pious Savanarola was executed by a Church commission for criticizing the papacy of the less than pious Alexander VI, who unlike Savanarola managed to die in bed with the last sacraments. Still, within the Christian body, "assent" to faith and "obedience" to hierarchy are the plain evidence of discipleship. The pastor's will may not be God's will, but it is God's will that we mean what we say when we say "Credo" and that we do what we are lawfully told to do. Catholics are most satisfied when their general well-being is ably represented and protected by pastors. Anything less can mean the presence of a sinful ecclesial situation, so commonplace in Italy at the time of Alexander VI's papacy.

Many Christian communities down the centuries were known mainly by their heresies and schisms. The apostolic complaints against both are fully developed in the New Testament's final Book of Revelation. There, St. John, within seventy years of the first Easter Sunday, speaks bluntly about seven new Churches in Asia Minor. Evildoing within the ranks is called "a curse", one said to merit inexorable punishment by God. The inspired writer speaks of the need for martyrs, proficient more in emptied self-will than in dialectics. Revelation charges the Church of Ephesus not to tolerate the wicked. It indicts as imposters those who assume the name "apostle" but betray its trust. "Do not be afraid of sufferings" was ordinary counsel to the early Christians of Smyrna; it warns against those in Thyatira who fail to uphold apostolic preaching and against those who commit adultery; the Laodiceans are challenged to be "hot or cold" (3:16): "But, because you are lukewarm, I will spit you out of my mouth." If people in our day take unkindly to such admonitions, it is for the reason that they are rarely exposed to such judgments anymore, even in the confessional for the few who still go. Recriminatory language in our time may be directed at greedy consumerists, warmongers, death-penalty advocates, those who do not pay their taxes or who discriminate in violation of civil law; but no longer do we make heretics and semi-heretics, adulterers, harlots, abortionists, or false worshippers uncomfortable about their sinful ways.

Whatever be the correct language suitable to a given period of

Church history, the contemporary problems of the American Church surely require a touch of biblical honesty. Lacking that, we may be guilty of the hypocrisy which drew so much fire from Christ. Making deals with the mammons of iniquity—whether they be popular irreligious trends or violence-prone anti-Churchmen, whether they be princes of the realm or of academe—has been a seamy side of the Church down the centuries.

The Church, humanly speaking, is no different from any other public institution. She has her share of special-interest groups, some of which enrich her life, some of which weaken it or tear it apart. In our time sociologists assign the label "veto group" to associations which amass enough power to deny legitimate rulers their rightful role as protectors of the body politic or as enforcers of public law. When ecclesial veto groups inhibit pastors from doing the right thing for their faithful, the Body of Christ becomes hostage to ecclesial terrorists, to those who use or threaten violence (often via the media) against the Church's shepherds. Not all leaders are capable of withstanding such opposition or of dying for the faith. More than that, the pretension of veto groups that, by confrontation, they help develop Catholic doctrine has not been verified in the post–Vatican II period, if the *Catechism of the Catholic Church* is the book of faith for the next century. For such a lack of contribution, the "veto groups" have inflicted a high degree of suffering on the faithful.

Let us return to another word used to justify the activity of veto groups—in monasteries, in classrooms, in seminaries, on campuses. The "freedom" popularly advertised in secular society is not the freedom of the sons of God, nor is it the freedom to do blatant wrong. In its French connection, it meant freedom, not only from a king, but from God and, a fortiori, from the Church which speaks for Christ. That people are free to leave the Church is a given of all modern societies; that they are free seriously to disrupt, disorient, or destroy the Church's security, mores, or vital laws, while claiming good standing on a par with the saints of

Sunday morning, is a claim not recognized by civil governments or by private voluntary associations either. If Charles Curran or Richard McCormick had done to the *New York Times,* or the AFL–CIO, or the NAACP, or to B'nai Brith, what they have done to the Church, they would have been fired in short order.

All kinds of disbelief and moral wrongdoing are discoverable within the Church's ranks. This is what the sufferings of Christ were all about. But the Church can never appear to give legitimacy to heresy or sin. John XXIII wanted a positive and optimistic Council, but he never intended to wipe out the difference between the good and bad Catholic. He prayed for mercy for unbelievers and sinners but did not abolish judgment about sin or sinners, either by God or by a pastor/confessor. He hoped that wives and husbands would always be faithful to each other but did not supersede Christ's warning about adultery, even when it is hidden in the heart.

In other words, *the Church cannot permit* too much social distance to exist between what she says and how she lives.

The Church cannot afford to call "original sin" a "fundamental" Christian doctrine yet permit important teachers to suggest it is little more than a primitive religious myth, not a necessary truth.

The Church cannot afford to speak of Christ as mankind's Redeemer, who saved the human race from its sinfulness, even as contemporary Catholic humanists describe him to the young mainly as a social reformer.

The Church cannot believe that Christ was born of Mary, ever a Virgin, while biblicists in episcopal centers suggest otherwise.

The Church cannot proclaim herself as the Church of Christ but coexist peacefully with scholars who teach seminarians and college students that Christ likely did not have a separate Church in mind.

The Church cannot describe her worship as a re-presentation of Christ's sacrifice on the Cross with salvific personal effects if at the parish level the stress is laid more on the community sense it generates than on its importance for sanctification.

The Church cannot speak of the Eucharist as Christ's Real Presence if adoration is neglected and irreverence or the unworthy reception of Holy Communion is allowed to become widespread.

The Church cannot insist on the reality of heaven, hell, and purgatory as essential elements of conscience formation if priests never preach of mortal sin or of its death-dealing effects.

The Church cannot define the sacrament of Penance as the ordinary means for the remission of sin if bishops do not insist on this preaching or make the judgment of internal states as much a matter of the sacrament as external reconciliation. Priests also cannot preach penance if they are not available for sacramental penance.

The Church cannot claim that the truth of her mission is guaranteed by bishops in union with the Pope if in practice the bishops do nothing to guarantee those truths of the Catechism which are regularly denied within their institutions.

The Church cannot assert, at a higher level, the rights and responsibility of the hierarchy to provide such guarantees if bishops denigrate the office of pastors at a lower level or permit pastors to disagree on catechetical content, even in the public forum.

The Church cannot laud the Fatherhood of God, or of her priests, if she permits feminists to disrespect the nature of both.

The Church cannot call upon divinely revealed moral absolutes as controlling factors for determining right Catholic behavior if major theological consultants for her many institutions/infrastructures are on public record as disbelieving the absoluteness of such postulates.

The Church cannot speak with integrity on religious life if in practice violations of the vows of poverty, chastity, or obedience go uncorrected over a long period.

The Church cannot speak of sexual morality at all if her approach to contraception, in or out of marriage, is timid, evasive, or allows preachers to treat such sexual sins as peccadillos.

The Church cannot speak of the sanctity of marriage if she does not lay stress on the importance of children to that sanctity.

The Church will never convince a skeptical age of the indissoluble nature of consummated Christian marriage if she appears to provide unconscionable divorces through her own annulment procedures.

The Church will hardly witness the holiness of Christian marriage as long as the asceticism expected of her priests and religious is not an exemplary witness.

The Church will scandalize her faithful if she seems more interested in politics than in holiness or if she seeks to impose prudential judgments as moral norms or usurps the proper role of the laity in the reform of secular institutions.

The *sensus fidei* of the Catholic Church calls for Catholics to be trained to "think with the Church", regardless of how they may live such formation out in practice. Such indoctrination, however, is not possible in a house divided against itself or in one which accepts as an operative principle that indoctrination is not its reason for existence. The Catholic faith has a unity or "wholeness" which precludes stripping away from its heart and soul any of the doctrines listed above. Obviously, disbelieving in Christ's divinity is a different form of heresy from disbelieving Mary to be the Mother of God. Still, "pick and choose" Catholicity, which John Paul II criticized so severely in his 1987 visit to the United States and is endemic to so many Catholic institutions, is heresy nonetheless. Fully believing Catholics know the difference and see, to their pain, the radical effect of selective faith on the lives of their children and grandchildren. Over twenty years ago, Notre Dame's historian Jay P. Dolan opined that, by the twenty-first century, the Catholic Church would follow the religious patterns developed earlier by Judaism and Protestantism, i.e., that she would be characterized by high, middle, and low Catholics. In point of fact, such existential divisions between practicing, tepid, and cultural but nonbelieving Catholics have always existed. But these categories have never been legitimized as desirable by Christ or the Church. The day that such a division appears to be legitimized in a Church which claims divine sanctions, the Catholic community will have lost its soul, and most of its people.

Sins against faith are, in the first instance, reserved to the judgment of conscience and, as needed, to the sacramental confessional process. However, from New Testament times, Church authority has moved against the most virulent scandalmongers in timely fashion, sometimes slowly, not infrequently after serious loss of membership. Defense of faith and morals has always been, however, an honorable exercise of episcopal or papal oversight, at least until modern times, when scholars and other independent Catholic spirits adopted a secular definition of their freedom to think as they will and teach or write accordingly. When, at the turn of the twentieth century, Pius X squelched the influence of Catholic Modernists within the Church, academics then and thereafter resented the censures. John Tracy Ellis assured me during the 1940s that Pius X would never be canonized a saint (he *was* in 1950), because of what he had done to academics—making them take an oath against Modernism, for one thing, and causing some of them to be fired. Indeed, a 1980 reviewer of *The Battle for the American Church* was surprised that any book in an enlightened era could speak of "religious" crime.

Following a summer teaching stint in 1952 at Catholic University, I confessed to my friend Ellis that the faculty members I met at the dinner table in Curley Hall were chronic complainers, suffering from an occupational disease known as "carping criticism". Behind me by that time were ten years of parish work, where one learned calmly to take slights and rebuffs as part of ordinary life. Academics, on the other hand, living in ivory towers, were sheltered somewhat from the real world. Many of them, holding down lifetime jobs protected by tenure, look upon rebuffs from superiors or inferiors as insults to their professional dignity. On the other hand, big-league scholars in the Church's public arena accepted with good grace ecclesial restraints on any speculations that might harm the good of souls. Jean Daniélou, Henri de Lubac, and Hans Urs von Balthasar went on to be named cardinals. There is a delicate balance here, to be sure. The freedom of any individual academic is not simply what an undisciplined theorist would like it to be but is subordinate to the freedom of the Church, through her hierarchy, to be true to herself. Censured academics, therefore, are not *ipso facto* blameless for the conduct that brought judgment on them.

Not surprisingly, those who protest the use of force against activity often become experts at using force against anyone who threatens their dominance or hegemony. In all the debates about Vatican II, about theological arguments, about what represents progress or retrogression for the Church, little attention has been paid to the antiestablishment hostility of many Catholic subleaders, sometimes Church officials themselves. Von Balthasar wrote at length of the anti-Roman virus prevalent in Europe's Catholic intellectual circles. But the animus extends far beyond that—against whatever represents tradition, or orthodoxy, or whatever comes from "on high", and against those who stand for those historic values. John Courtney Murray, who in 1941 was upholding Jesuits as a model of fidelity for New York priests, denied to this writer, two weeks before he died, that he could make that claim in 1967. By then Murray himself was facing antipathy from younger Jesuits who considered him a "traditionalist". Still, he suffered through frustrations of his own and could be quoted as saying: "Some people say the American bishops should lead; I'm not too sure— after all, who knows where they would lead?"[1]

The history of the past twenty-five years is a story of repressive force used to dilute, deform, or stonewall the full Catholic message

[1] Peter Hebblethwaite, *The Runaway Church* (1975), p. 13.

and to isolate or punish those who insist on its preachment, and especially on its institutionalization. Catholic apologists may not always be nice people, but even the most judicious and saintly of them have lost positions, promotions, and salary increases in the Catholic press, in colleges, seminaries, and diocesan offices simply because they preached the Church message precisely the way it was given—or opposed, even in gentlemanly fashion, distortions of that message.

This is still "the Battle" that Church authority continues to lose, as much in 1994 as in 1978.

The Church has a new universal Catechism because a synod of the world's bishops in 1985, led by Boston's Cardinal Bernard Law, with John Paul II concurring, decided that so widespread was the confusion among the faithful on matters of faith and morals, brought on by irresponsible, often dissenting, academics, that a codified restatement of the Catholic faith and its priorities was absolutely necessary to reestablish the credibility of the Church herself. Catholic intelligentsia, on the other hand (in the words of one of their numbers), "caught up in the general drift of secular opinion, tend to espouse positions considerably more permissive and ecumenically open than those of many senior pastors (bishops, monsignors, and the like) or those of the run-of-the-pew Catholic". This is currently true, and few will dispute their legitimate freedom. But the abuses have been so widespread, down to "the run-of-the-pew Catholic" via "the run-of-the-classroom teacher", that in self-defense Church authority has finally moved to draw lines for the responsible free exercise of Catholic thinking. Intelligentsia, therefore, particularly those who belong to any one of the Church's "veto groups", are now situated between their desire for unlimited free speech and "the law" of the truly Catholic mind. Church authority has begun to seek ways of bringing its teaching and formation processes into conformity with the obligations inherent in sincere and honestly professed Catholic commitment.

American bishops faced a similar difficulty in 1884 at the Third

Plenary Council of Baltimore after they authorized a Baltimore Catechism. If, today, one reads biographies of important prelates of that period like James Cardinal Gibbons, Archbishop John Ireland, or Archbishop Michael Corrigan, he finds the subject of a Baltimore Catechism mentioned but hardly the focus of special attention subsequent to its authorization. The Catechism was simply written, promulgated, and transmitted. While theologians were consulted—and a few, even then, did not like Catholicity reduced to propositions—Gibbons (the Council's apostolic delegate) appreciated their efforts but made it clear that they were working under the bishops. The subject of the translation of the Baltimore Catechism into other languages arose almost simultaneously but died just as quickly when San Antonio's Archbishop Neraz intervened to say that the Mexicans of the Southwest already had a Spanish catechism, and one more translation would only confuse them.

More important, perhaps, for the effectiveness of that Baltimore meeting than an official text of authentic catechetical propositions was the effort by those bishops to secure a better governance of the Church's machinery so that content of that text would be transmitted faithfully. Historian Peter Guilday summarized well the ecclesiastical disorder of the earlier nineteenth-century Church— "priests who knew not how to obey", "laity who were interpreting their share of Catholic life by non-Catholic norms", "misrule" and "incompetence" in major sees. Apparently the principal need of the American Church during this high point of her American development was discipline among her priests and teachers. This was what the bishops proceeded to initiate in 1884 with 319 decrees: clerical dress for priests, religious habits for those vowed to community life, norms of behavior for both, rules on sacramental life, parochial schools, the proposal of a university, better supervision of pastors and religious communities, and so forth. Although cries against episcopal overmanagement would be heard from anti-Romanists and Americanizing critics of Church authority well into the twentieth century (some of which led to the chiding of "Americanism" by Leo XIII in 1899), the discipline invoked by bishops in 1884 worked. American priests and religious became numerous, respected, and respectable, anticlericalism hardly existed, and American Catholics had few equals in the world for their knowledge of the faith and their personal piety. The bishops themselves were respectful of Rome's universal jurisdiction. Within limits, they modified universal directives to meet American needs, but only with the Pope's approval and a warning from Gibbons that if bishops did not accommodate the Holy See, they might receive demands they did not like.

Indeed, the Pastoral Letter of the Third Plenary Council ended on this ringing note:

> The spirit of American freedom is not one of anarchy or license. It essentially involves love of order, respect for rightful authority and obedience to just laws. There is nothing in the character of the most liberty-loving American, which could hinder his reverential submission to the Divine Authorities of Our Lord, or to the like authority delegated to His Apostles and His Church. Nor are there in the world more devoted adherents of the Catholic Church, the See of Peter, and the Vicar of Christ, than the Catholics of the United States. . . . We glory that we are, and with God's blessing shall continue to be, not the American Church, nor the Church of the United States, nor a Church in any sense exclusive or limited, but an integral part of the one, holy, Catholic and apostolic Church of Jesus Christ.

The new *Catechism of the Catholic Church* may be a teaching document, but it is not self-executing. Good teaching is more than the recitation of words, and good learning results more from good order in the teaching situation than from entertaining speech. In the Catechism's case, right conviction and appropriate behavior are the desired results. The centrifugal forces which could have threatened the execution of the Baltimore Catechism are today much more powerful, much more entrenched, much more terrorist-minded than the earlier critics of things *magisterial;* and contemporary bishops (as well as Rome) are more unsure than those in 1884 of how authoritative they should or can be. But to be authoritative properly one must first know that about which one must be authoritative; second, one must know how to command and gain compliance; and third, one must have the good sense to know when persuasion fails and sanctions against the unruly must begin. Good people do not need many sanctions (1 Tim 3:8), and good governance involves sound political judgment not only about social (ecclesial) good and evil but also about how to keep the balance on the side of the good.

The bishops of 1884 knew that priests and religious could create most of their difficulties, so they directed their attention to their training and discipline. James McMasters and Orestes Brownson were at times hairshirts to the hierarchy, but these laymen merely wanted bishops to be good at what they were supposed to do. Catholics at every station of life also respected Rome's universal jurisdiction. And the American bishops of those days went on to build a remarkable corpus of infrastructures, in the words of Bishop Gerald Shaughnessy, a Church "better than they knew".

It was these institutional arrangements—colleges, religious orders, academic institutions—that became vulnerable to the free-wheeling spirit following Vatican II, when Catholic leaders undertook to move in a direction entirely contrary to that laid down in 1884, indeed, inconsistent with the documents of 1965. The Catholic Church still lives off that life conceptualized and nurtured in 1884, but the "autonomy" against Church authority, eschewed by bishops and laity in the nineteenth century, is now commonplace in Catholic parishes, schools, even in diocesan headquarters. The extent of "pick and choose" Catholicity—a form of heresy identified with Martin Luther—is verifiable in many Catholic places.

If bishops in union with the Pope, at the onset of the twenty-first century, do not insist on what the bishops in the twentieth century claimed as their prerogative, then the new Catechism will become a dead letter. If bishops with one voice cannot say about their people, their academics, and each other today what bishops said then, we are dealing with a major Catholic evil. The work of minimizing the Catechism's importance and relevance is already in progress, sometimes orchestrated by academics who claim episcopal favor.

Chapter Three

Post–Vatican II Challenges to the Doorkeepers of Heaven

Pio Laghi was not long in his office on Massachusetts Avenue when a college president from the country's heartland thought it might be a nice idea for the new apostolic delegate to lecture on his Midwest campus. The offer was pleasantly received, but the educator was surprised at the final word, which went something like this: "I'd better stay close to home. My predecessor created more than a hundred bishops, and I have to do something about that."

The diplomat was referring to his predecessor, Archbishop Jean Jadot, sent to Washington, D.C., by Paul VI after the Council (1973–1980) and who, although he earned high marks from the Church's "progressive" forces, ended up out of favor in Rome. Jadot today has retired to his native Belgium, the only apostolic delegate to the United States ever to be denied the cardinalate on his return. He was a creature of Belgium's Cardinal Suenens, who also found himself in disfavor for espousing causes that proved harmful to the Pope.

By 1980, Archbishop Laghi's sailing orders presumed that bishops, and the new body of bishops in particular, were part of the Church's burgeoning institutional problem. The original difficulties grew out of the Council itself and were compounded by Rome's watchful waiting. The Holy See, however, hoped to alleviate these difficulties through better diplomatic relations with national episcopal conferences and the appointment of bishops more in tune with the mind of Paul VI than that of Cardinal Suenens. Initially, these episcopal bodies were set up without guidelines and, until it was almost too late, without close supervision by the Pope.

Rome should have known better, if only from its long history of difficulties with hierarchies going back to the fourth century: throughout the years of the Avignon Captivity and the sellout of Rome by German and English bishops during the Protestant revolt. Even John XXIII's own Council turned out to be somewhat anti-Roman. Leading Continental cardinals, sometimes called "the Belgian Bloc" because of rump meetings held on that soil, turned the Council away from the original intentions of the Pope and his Curia. Ralph Wiltgen's *The Rhine Flows into the Tiber* (1966) described that turnabout in great detail. Although the final Vatican II documents are Catholic to the core, the spirit engendered by the political infighting from 1962 to 1965 was not always felicitous, forcing the diplomatic Paul VI to use papal muscle at times to keep it in line with John XXIII's real objectives.

Subsequently, a certain spirit of autonomy developed within the world's hierarchies, which, by the time of Laghi's arrival in 1980, was enhanced by new "Jadot" bishops. The American hierarchy had been more or less pro-Roman from its early days, even though there were occasional tugs-of-war over specific adaptations of universal Catholic policies. Bishops in the nineteenth century not infrequently fought their battles in the secular press, and the line-up of contesting views occasionally pitted Baltimore vs. Rome or New York, or St. Paul vs. Rochester, or Peoria vs. Chicago. Others besides members of the episcopal club knew who was on what side. Still, during, and after, all these shouting matches, no doubt existed in anyone's mind about what it meant to be Catholic or about who really was running the Church.

Even though Rome was wary at first of the National Catholic Welfare Conference, created after World War I, the bureaucracy set up at 1312 Massachusetts Avenue in the nation's Capitol was by and large Rome-conscious. If the staff there recognized the Pope's primacy of jurisdiction, so did their bishop leaders and bishops-in-the-field. In addition, the NCWC had no direct power over bishops, who disagreed at times with NCWC leadership and with each other. Some bishops were "small" in ecclesial influence, while others, by virtue of the sees they administered, were "big". Yet, big or small, a given bishop rarely hesitated to pick up a phone to tell the general secretary what he thought of his policy or activity, or to chastise a staff priest for interfering in his diocese. Nor would it surprise the properly informed that some bishops often said: "I pay my diocesan dues to the NCWC so that I can ignore them." The machinery of the National Office was generally controlled by leading archbishops from the Midwest (more or less Chicago, Detroit, Cincinnati), but the cardinals of Philadelphia, New York, and Boston, who represented the East, where half of all Catholic Americans then lived, were independent voices, having large influence in Rome. (That balance of influence no longer exists, certainly not in public perception.)

At a time when enlightened political opinion was well organized in civic affairs against "states' rights", judging that to be a hypocritical cover for citizens wishing to disobey "the law of the land", Catholic elites, first in Europe, began to argue "local Church rights" against Rome. The Catholic Church may stand for a universal revealed Word of God and an objective moral order everywhere, but certain intelligentsia sought to have the message particularized, relativized, culturized. Breaking Rome's hold on universal definitions and discipline was one way to gain their objective. John XXIII sensed this before he died. He wondered among his friends how to call the Council off. Two years after the Council's end, the First Synod of the world's bishops directed national hierarchies to deal correctively with what would have been heresy or public immorality to earlier generations. The decree of the Synod was ignored.

Undeniably, the centrifugal tendencies of modern society became virulent forces within the Catholic community, especially in the established Churches of the West. The first national body to rebel against Rome's primacy of jurisdiction was the Dutch Church, sparked by her university professors and abetted by the hierarchy. Today, the once proud Catholicity of Holland is but a shadow of its pre–World War II self. Thirty years later, mid-European theologians, not excluding some prominent bishops, continue to criticize Rome for its preoccupation with doctrine, when its major business should be uplifting the poor; in 1993, three German bishops, two of whom are closely associated with Cardinal Ratzinger, suggested (in contradiction to John Paul II) that pastors be allowed on their own to determine when Catholics in invalid marriages can receive the Eucharist worthily. In Australia, the strain between *Romanitá* bishops and others is beginning to show in public. Many of their prominent but dissenting academics, often protected by bishops there, were trained in American Catholic colleges. Even in Ireland some religionists would blur Catholic distinctiveness, if only to further union with the Protestant North.

In 1985, in the home of a Vatican official, the question was raised whether a schism within the United States were possible. The cardinal interjected immediately: "No, there are too many practicing Catholics and faithful clergy there. But in Brazil, at least half the hierarchy is on a dangerous anti-Roman course."

Deviation from Catholic norms is now widespread in the West, although there are some among the African elite, too, who find no inconsistency between Christianity and some form of polygamy. In other countries, critics of this distressing status quo blame "the loss of faith", "breakdown of morals", "catechesis without content", "clerical and religious misbehavior", etc., for the disorder. But for American Catholics of this century, an unruly Church is a new experience. Historian Peter Guilday attributed Catholic impiety in the early nineteenth century to a lack of discipline among our clergy and incompetence in high places. These arguments are sometimes made today. Discipline, the liberating force in any society, which helps produce first-rate surgeons, record-breaking runners, and saintly priests, has clearly gone. "Discipline", which for rugged individualists conjures up images of torture and the rack, is merely an assembly of good habits acquired by doing good things time and time again, often under someone's direction. Not without some pain at first, but in due course almost effortlessly.

Before the specifics of the American "Battle" come under review, it is necessary to say a few things about the constitution of the Church.

The *magisterium* of the Church, in its official documents, says three things about itself:

1. *The Church is hierarchical,* i.e., she, her holy message, and the guarantee of gospel truth come "from above". Human rationality and experience enflesh what has been given by God, just as Mary's body once enfleshed the Son of God. But the people of God are not headless, and they do not create the message nor guarantee its truth.

2. *The Church is authoritative,* i.e., she is governed by a pope, universally by bishops in union with him, and at the local level by pastors in union with the bishop. All the power Christ claimed from the Father he bestowed as the "power of the keys to heaven" on Peter and his apostles. And thereby on their successors. This power is legislative, judicial, and executive. In effect, the Church's shepherds proclaim what God's law is, what it means in the concrete, and see to it that the revealed Word, including its Commandments, vivify the Church's daily life, especially within the institutions of her own household.

3. *The Church is paternal,* i.e., the pastors of the Church are men who have the fatherly role to guide, protect, and govern the people of God in Christ's name.

All of these propositions are rejected by modern political writers, even within the Church. Dissenters point to abuses inherent in one-man rule of any kind, asserting instead the necessity of checks and balances, of divided authority structures, and of plebiscites, if only to keep officials responsible to the people. This commentary would stray far afield if it were to debate this issue in depth. In free societies, citizens do have voting power, but in modern practice this may be the sum of their democratic input. Modern states are often in the control of special interests, of combines of special interests, and occasionally of mini-mobs. De facto, bureaucracies manage society's daily doings with little reference to the will of the people. "Open covenants openly arrived at" may have been a Woodrow Wilson dream, but they never truly reflected what went on in Washington, D.C., or later in the League of Nations or in the United Nations.

In the Catholic tradition, there is nothing per se wrong with hierarchy, authority, democracy—or paternalism—as long as the rule of reason prevails and the law of God, more or less, is operative. The Church, which is answerable only to Christ, has her own checks and balances, and the "father" who runs his house like an autocrat eventually will be subject to judgment. The father who does not have his hand on the pulse of his people is also worse than a fool. But, so is the father who bows to the foolishness of special interests within the household, which do harm to all who live within. Every virtue, of course, has its down side, fortitude tends to masochism, mercy to weakness. Still, the sternness of some fathers (and mothers) is no reason to extirpate parenthood, any more than unruly children are the justification for derogating the authority of fathers and mothers. Ruling involves lordship or ladyship. It denotes domination which for good reason is exercised rightfully, and properly, and chiefly, by those elected or named to high office. Incompetence, malfeasance, or tyranny must be handled by every society in its own fashion. The Church does not always do this well, but secular society, which no longer acknowledges the Lordship of Christ, is hardly the Church's paradigm.

Furthermore, Church politics, which surely exists, should revolve around right and wrong, truth and error, good and bad, not power. Yet, in the volatile culture of Modernity, power politics is the name of the game. A biblicist speaks of the doctrinal definition that *won out* at Nicaea or Trent; a moralist discussing contraception bases his views on "the will of the people"; the nonordination of women priests is reducible, in the minds of certain dogmatists, to male "haves" unwilling to share status with female "have-nots". When sacred matters are alleged to be mere cases of progress or reaction, liberalism vs. conservatism, somehow truth and right, even God, are lost in the process.

But the cause of Church authority as the guardian of God's Word is not helped either:

— IF bishops are embarrassed at being the hierarchy.

— IF bishops are not one with each other or with the Pope about what is truly Catholic.

— IF bishops criticize the Pope's Curia publicly and the Pope's policies on Catholic worship or doctrine vicariously.

— IF bishops stonewall the implementation of universal norms or speak as if they by their own will are dispensed from universal norms.

— IF bishops lend comfort to dissent and disobedience among priests and religious by including one or the other in their apparatus or by remaining silent in the face of repeated offenses against Church law.

— IF bishops use authority selectively, mostly against critics of dissent or against defenders of the *magisterium* primarily.

— IF bishops appear in public as strong spokesmen for Catholic teaching or policies but work privately, sometimes in Roman circles, to mute the impact of Church statements on their dissident constituencies.

—IF bishops, while not denying Catholic doctrine or its relevancy to Christian life, express so much understanding of sinful behavior that the perpetrators develop a sense of righteousness with no sense of the need of conversion.

The proper use of authority means that responsible Church officers within their jurisdiction conduct Catholic affairs according to law and the legislated policy of the Church. Vatican II was not yet complete when an old hand at the Catholic University of America demonstrated how this can be done effectively but without bombast. Sulpician Louis Arand, president of Divinity College there for many years, was greeted in December 1965 by a group of priests on campus who expressed the intention of concelebrating Mass according to the newly approved *Constitution on the Sacred Liturgy.* Fr. Arand reminded them that diocesan guidelines were lacking, since the archbishop was still in Rome. The young priests countered with the observation that they felt free in conscience to do so immediately. Fr. Arand's final word came effortlessly: "I've a great regard for your conscience, having taught you what you know about it. But it is well for you to remember that my conscience sets the policy for worship in this university under the archbishop. There will be no concelebration here until he says when and how." The priests did not dare do otherwise.

The American Scene

American bishops played no significant role in the Council, save perhaps on the Church-state issue and, to a lesser degree, on matters liturgical. Nonetheless, many of them were caught up in the turmoil and in public anti-Roman politicking for the first time. In the 1960s this was heady stuff. They also brought or ran into academics who were more aggressive away from home and more adept in controversy and media coverage than they were. John Courtney Murray was a quiet stream of conversation compared to the gushing waterfall that was Francis X. Murphy (Xavier Rynne). The would-be changemakers in the American hierarchy, who were not necessarily more classically libertarian in management style than the ones frequently cited as authoritarian, received sympathetic attention from *Time* and *Newsweek,* and from *Herder's Correspondence* and *NCNews,* too. Other American bishops, content with the state of the American Church, felt "If it's not broke, don't fix it." But the mood of the decade was not in their favor.

However, it is clear in hindsight that cultural unhappiness outside the Church had taken root within, even as early as the 1950s, and among important populations. Most visibly unhappy were the opinion-molders, those observers of, rather than players in, the institutional life of country or Church. Joseph Becker's *The Re-Formed Jesuits* (1992) cites chapter and verse about the upheavals going on in the Society of Jesus, with few outsiders knowing that early the extent of a religious revolution in the making. John Tracy Ellis' *American Catholics and Intellectual Life* (1956), originally an article of oversimplifications, stirred up Catholic college professors with the charge that the Church, by repressing their creativity, was not helpful in producing acceptable or recognized scholars. This was said at the very time when the Catholic educational system was growing, gaining respect, and, by its obvious strength, creating not a little anxiety among anti-Catholic elites. Neil McCluskey, who left the Jesuit priesthood after the Council, published (in 1970) a catalogue of the Church's sins against academics called *The Catholic University: A Modern Appraisal.* By and large, however, these were more occupational complaints than the promotion of doctrinal or moral deviance, the kind commonplace in academic circles today.

Such stirrings before the Council would bubble afterward into storms far more serious for the Church. The evidence for how this came to be has been amply compiled, but for the purpose of this review only two authors and two books will be singled out for the radical impact they had on run-of-the-mill Catholics, clergy included: Avery Dulles' *Models of the Church* (1974) and Raymond Brown's *Priest and Bishop* (1970). In *Models,* Dulles, who once attributed his Catholic conversion to the lack of a *magisterium* in the Church of his youth, considered the institutional model of the Church (the only Church Catholics know) as the least important model of Christ's Church in the post–Vatican II ecumenical world. In this book he developed a line of thought which enervated the adherence that American Catholics had come to accept as binding for members of "the one, true" Church: The Church as an institution, he says, has "a comparatively meager basis in scripture and in early Church tradition" (p. 179).

Perhaps the significant paragraph is worth citing in full:

> This ecclesiology is out of phase with the demands of the times. In an age of dialogue, ecumenism, and interest in world religions, the monopolistic tendency of this model is unacceptable. In an age when all large institutions are regarded with suspicion or aversion, it is exceptionally difficult to attract people to a religion that represents itself as primarily institutional. As sociologists have noted we are experiencing in our age the breakdown of closed societies. While people are willing to dedicate themselves to a cause or a movement, they do not wish to bind themselves totally to any institution. Institutions are seen as self-serving and repressive, and as needing to be kept under strong vigilance. In our modern pluralistic society, especially in a country such as the United States, people do not experience any given Church as a necessary means of giving significance to their lives. But they may prefer a certain Church as providing services that could not equally be found elsewhere. Fulfillment and significance are things that an individual usually finds more in private than in the public sphere, more in the personal, than in the institutional.[1]

Apart from the use of words like "primarily", "closed", or "monopoly", which the Church never uses in her apologetic, the

[1] Read pp. 188–91; also pp. 40 and 187 especially.

Dulles reasoning, even if in his case he was speaking only abstractly, was not what Christ used when he called for faith in him and when he set up the apostolic college in the real world. But the cynicism against the Church institution became influential in seminaries, convents, and college classrooms. It became the basis of the headless "people of God's Church", so popular after Vatican II, and of that "double *magisterium* of Dulles" which made bold to suggest that bishops ought not to issue formal doctrinal proclamations without clearing them with his theological community.

The Vatican II document *The Dogmatic Constitution on the Church* devoted more space to the episcopacy and the priesthood—one quarter of the text—than to any other aspect of Catholicity. In doing so, the Council reiterated what the Church has proclaimed about her divine institution from her earliest days. Through the religious controversies following Nicaea (325), the debates of the early and late Middle Ages concerning lay investiture, the sixteenth-century difficulties with the Sacrifice of the Mass and the Eucharist, and later at Trent and at Vatican I, the Church has looked upon doubts about the institutionalization of the Pope's primacy, the episcopacy, and the priesthood as doubts about the nature of Christ's message.

Yet, in *Priest and Bishop,* Raymond Brown, from his academic world, asserts (he would say "on historical grounds alone") that Jesus instituted neither the priesthood nor the episcopacy as such. The New Testament does not speak of priests, he avers (p. 13), and we cannot presume that those who presided at the early Eucharists were priests or that they looked upon the Eucharist as a sacrifice (p. 16). About bishops and Peter, he says the following:

> The presbyter-bishops described in the New Testament were not in any traceable way successors of the Twelve Apostles. . . . They succeeded in the sense that they came later. To say that

the episcopate was divinely established or established by Christ can be defended only if one says it emerged under the guidance of the Holy Spirit (pp. 72, 73).

There is no real proof that in the New Testament times Peter would have been looked on as a bishop of the Roman community. . . . The functions of the Twelve end up in the hands of Peter's successor, but this concentration produces the difficulties we now encounter in Catholicism (pp. 79, 80).

By the time Brown was writing these views, his reference group was no longer St. Mary's Catholic Seminary in Baltimore but the interdenominational Union Theological Seminary in New York, where such views of Catholic origins were commonplace. He once called his exegesis "detective work", and so it is. But he reminds many of the detective who fell upon an old building in whose cellar there were a number of "baby" records—birth certificates, immigration and naturalization papers, a father's diary, and some artifacts—from which he speculated extensively, not only about the nationality and economic status of the family's members, but of its genetic potential. That same detective never bothered to find out that the family which was the subject of his speculation now lived in the next town and was better qualified than he to tell what those "baby" documents meant. Similarly, the New Testament is the Church's "baby" document. The living Church is better qualified to define the origins of her papacy, episcopacy, and priesthood than an observer who, looking at a baby picture—and nothing else—decides that the adult who finally appeared must be an intruder.

While many priests, and not a few literate laity, were upset by *Priest and Bishop,* the book was distributed free of charge to rectories around the country with episcopal permission. When Chicago's John Cardinal Cody found himself the recipient of cartons of this book, he sent an analysis of its content, prepared under his direction, to Baltimore to Lawrence Cardinal Shehan, Brown's bishop and at whose major seminary the biblicist taught for years. Shehan took the Chicago critique seriously enough to rebut Brown personally, if belatedly, the only major bishop since Vatican II to criticize in scholarly fashion and in detail an academic's faulty theorizing.[2]

To Brown's theory that the Holy Spirit seventy years after Christ, not Christ himself, founded the episcopacy, the priesthood, and the Sacrifice of the Mass, Cardinal Shehan countered with good questions:

> Where was the influence of the Holy Spirit when the original traditions were being formed among the early Christians? When the Gospels and other works of the New Testament were being written? When the canon of the New Testament was being formed? When the general Councils, including Trent, Vatican I and Vatican II, were making their decisions for the Church?

Shehan was really asking: How could the Holy Spirit have been so wrong, so long, if Brown is right?

While Brown rejected all criticism of his theories as arch-conservative obscurantism, one would think that his views, like those of Dulles and McCormick, as much as those of Charles Curran or Richard McBrien, would have received prompt overview. On the contrary, Brown, more than any of the others, was provided with unique platforms (e.g., at conventions of the National Catholic Educational Association) from which to lash out at conservatives and arch-conservatives, claiming that they were trying to intimidate the Catholic hierarchy. The truth, if there be such a thing as demonstrable historical truth, may well have been the contrary. Unquestionably, the most influential voices in the post–Vatican II Church on the public opinion of Catholics, from the simplest laity and clergy to their wisest counterparts, have been those who theorized against traditional Catholic understandings of who Christ was and what he meant or intended.

Thirty years after the Council, public figures as varied as Hans

[2] *Homiletic and Pastoral Review,* January 1976.

Küng, Rosemary Reuther, and Margaret Steinfels freely admit
that the innovators took early charge of the Church's thinking
processes. Within ten years of the Council's beginning, a man who
left the priesthood to create the now defunct National Association
of the Laity asserted boldly that "liberals" have "gained control of
the Roman Catholic Church in America". T. Joseph O'Donoghue
defined the coup in this fashion:

> Liberal Catholics have a locktight grip on the publication of
> catechisms and religious formation texts, and a similarly tight
> grip on university religious education departments, which train
> religious teachers at all levels. Liberal Catholics have mastered
> the techniques of designing structures and liaison patterns to
> multiply total impact. Pity the poor establishment, which sees
> the once docile Catholic populace of its area now constantly
> infused by liberal itinerants whose words endure in small but
> solid local liberal movements.[3]

That old establishment called Mother Church may have more
recovery power than the ex-Father O'Donoghue thought. But
unquestionably, and inexplicably, the implications of what the
Browns, the Dulleses, and the McCormicks were saying everywhere seemed to delude many, especially those in high places.
Only recently (1993), Dulles told a meeting of bishops that adherence or nonadherence to the basic teaching of *Humanae vitae*
ought not to be a litmus test for the appointment of future
bishops. But why make only this an exception to the credal
fidelity expected of all successors to the apostles? In responding to
John Paul II's *Veritatis splendor,* Richard McCormick indicated that
in defending moral absolutes, the Pope misunderstands moralists
like himself. How is it possible ever to come to grips with moral
relativists within the Catholic establishment if, by reinterpreting
words, they still claim authenticity?

Fr. Brown goes one step farther. Back in March 1981, he wrote

[3] *National Catholic Reporter,* March 24, 1972.

an article for *Theological Studies* entitled "Scriptures as the Word of God". It was vintage Brown, the academic, abstracted from the real world of the Church. What interests most is how he downgrades all the Church's most solemn statements about Holy Writ, even Vatican II's declaration that "the Books of Scripture must be acknowledged as teaching firmly, faithfully, and without error that truth which God put into the sacred writings for the sake of our salvation" (*Dei Verbum,* no. 11).

This formula, he says, was merely a "face-saving device" to placate conservatives at the Council. For him, the meaning of the assertion is still ambiguous. Popes presumptively are moving toward his views, Brown contends, even as they requote "with praise" past papal statements which they no longer believe to be true. Brown is much more radical than McCormick, even more so than Dulles. Fr. Dulles hedges his bets somewhat when he offers his models, not as "doctrinal theology, but for dialectic". He knows that "dialectic" is ongoing and open-ended discussion with a view to developing new hypotheses, theoretically unending and inconclusive. Chesterton once remarked that the open mind is like the open mouth; it must close on something solid. Not, however, for the dialectician in the Hegelian mold, who can keep conversations going endlessly without affirming anything as surely true. In *Models,* Dulles disavows he is doing "doctrinal theology"; he is merely dialoguing with his peers. But by writing in the popular media, he writes over the heads of bishops who (in theory at least) must deal in "doctrinal theology", on which faith in Christ depends. The end result of Dulles is an uncertain Church.

Fr. Brown's hypothesis that popes are with him, in spite of their official declarations, has infested Catholic public opinion with the suspicion already alive in some quarters that the *magisterium* has a hidden agenda. The present intellectual confusion is permitted to continue, it is said, because in high Church places there is uncertainty about traditional Catholic understandings of Christ's divinity, Mary's virginity, the nature of Christ's redemptive work, the priesthood, Real Presence, marital indissolubility, and so forth.

Hans Küng was only the first to tell audiences to discern the Church of the future by observing what Rome or the bishop does, not by attending to what either says. Even some bishops wonder how firmly Rome will defend the words of the new Catechism. The end result of permitting such wondering to grow would be the kind of religious body that Christ branded as hypocritical.

An occasional bishop may tell intimates that priests and religious have become more of a problem to the future of the Church than the unsettled laity, a judgment many laity already make. Yet, rare is it that any particular Catholic subgroup assumes for itself responsibility for the Catholic malaise which goes beyond personal sin or low morale. Certainly, the Church's academic opinion-molders, who de facto have acquired more influence over the formation of Catholic consciences than bishops, never seem to accept blame for the Church's doctrinal and moral malfunctioning. Unusual, too, is the episcopal body which has convicted its worst offenders of sinful behavior.

Without underestimating the real challenges that now beset a hierarchy that has watched the Church's unity disintegrate, under pressure from within as from without, the issue to be joined is not alleged conservatism or liberalism but what Vatican II called "the obedience of faith" (Rom 16:26). It is disobedience against the faith that is undermining Catholic vitality. How does the hierarchy restore that? Catholic faith calls for the acceptance of God's revealed truth on the basis of the witness given first by Christ and now by his Church's teaching office, faithfully proclaiming his teaching. Neither personal experience, nor empirical studies, nor deductive reasoning, nor reigning cultural expression—apart from or against Christ or the Church's wisdom—are witnesses to God's Word. However, the "obedience of faith" is a gift. And how to reclaim it, when it has been lost, is humanly speaking a puzzlement.

One thing is certain, however: disobedience against the faith begins with disrespect for the Church's teaching office which, when institutionalized within the household, only weakens the commitment of those with little faith, while scandalizing those whose faith is deeply rooted. Are bishops on top of what goes on within institutions chartered to bear the name Catholic? A thorough survey of institutional behavior would be very revealing, but a random sample of opinion in a variety of scholarly places, let alone in popular journals, should disturb more than a few bishops.

That theologian cited earlier, who takes for granted that the Catholic intelligentsia nowadays will always be "more permissive and ecumenically open than many senior pastors or the run-of-the-mill Catholic", opined further on the subject of Church authority in our time as follows:

— "We live in a time when the *magisterium* of popes and bishops carries very little weight with the vast majority of Catholics."

— "No thinking person can achieve honest certitude by accepting every human document, regardless of its relative solemnity and of its theological quality, as though it were the very Word of God."

— "The faithful are nowhere admonished to live by official doctrine alone."[4]

Any one of these propositions, articulated in this case by a respected theologian more than fifteen years ago, might be fairly discussed to discover whatever element of truth might lie in it. But, together, they manifest a sneering attitude toward "truth" proclaimed by authority and convey an unwarranted insinuation that somehow, especially in our day, the intelligentsia are the guardians of run-of-the-pew Catholics against the "cheap truth"

---

[4] Avery Dulles, S.J., "A Response—Certainty in the Catholic Church", *Long Island Catholic,* December 9, 1976.

not infrequently transmitted by Church headquarters. In a class-room or in a diocesan newspaper (where the above citations appeared), the eventual impact on the "obedience of faith" is negative.

In a healthy Catholic climate, therefore, "thinking with the Church", i.e., having "the mind of Jesus Christ" (Phil 2:5), is, or should be, the normal attribute of the believing Catholic, even if he has a Ph.D. Free-thinking within the parameters of the faith can be, and often has been, as wild as a sports contest, as fiery as a war that goes beyond words. Good Catholic debate, however, always respects the *magisterium* and the Church's chief witnesses to the teaching of the faith. It never causes (or should never cause) public scandal, even when, in a given case, a particular debater is injudiciously or incorrectly restrained by the criticism of Church authority. This happenstance is the condition of living in a civilized, to say nothing of a religious, society. Procedures of redress in such cases are far easier to find than remedies for the harm caused to souls by irresponsible or anti-Catholic behavior within institu-tions or by faculty members who ostensibly, one would think, profess fidelity to the Church.

The demythologizers of the Church's confessional statements have done their work well. Many Catholics today, not excluding some clergy, think their religious life might be better off without those fairy tales—about Virgin births, miracles, and supernatural demands from on high—all unprovable by modern methods of study. Fables manufactured by saints and scholars from the pre-scientific period of religious history can, they insist, no longer underpin popular belief or piety. Thus far, however, the demytho-logizing has gone only one way—against Judaeo-Christianity. Critical scholars do not manifest the same cynicism about the confessional statements of the secularist Church, presently insti-tutionalized in college classrooms: God is dead, dying, or undemon-strable; only empirical knowledge acquired by research is truth; the scientific method determines the quality of teaching and learning; nature evolves according to its own sequences, and so does truth; freedom is virtue; academic authority is a surer guide to the salvation of the world than the authority of Church and state; and so forth.

These propositions are in fact undemonstrable theories, however widespread their fideistic acceptance may be and however far-reaching their influence on the thought patterns of America's chief opinion-molders. Tragically, the secularist uncertainties have become gospel for Catholic academicians, often against the faith certainties of the Church's creeds.

Granted that any society—which successfully forms a real community of people—has its heroes, its sagas, and its dirges, which acquire a certain binding power beyond the identity and truth which make people a community in the first place. But the sagas of the Bible, like the miracles of Christ, are no less worthy of credibility than the myths which underpin the confessions and creeds of the secularist state or its various infrastructures. If the secular university wishes to operate out of a confessional worldview of its own, and to enforce this on those who subject themselves to it, there is no reason at all why the Christian or Jewish or Muslim university may not do likewise, in the name of freedom and the search for truth, which secularists call elusive.

If the Church is to be at the street level what she says she is in her documents, this is the situation with which Rome and national hierarchies must deal affirmatively.

Chapter Four

First Shepherds of the Flock in Conference

"According to Thomas J. Reese, S.J."

An outside review in 1994 of the management of the American Church by the National Conference of Catholic Bishops (NCCB) since 1966 ought, first, to take note of the "inside" analysis done in 1992 by Fr. Thomas J. Reese, a Jesuit professor at Georgetown University. Not without significance, *Shepherds of the Flock* was based, by the author's own confession, on his free access to the NCCB's personnel and documents, on other documents, too, which were leaked to him by friendly bishops, once Reese discovered he "could not get [them] from the NCCB/USCC staff". A reader need not be dissuaded about the book's importance by the fact that it was published under the auspices of the National Catholic Reporter Publishing Company, even though this sponsorship does offer a clue to the mind-set of the author and his informants. Both are satisfied, in general, with the present state of Catholic procedures; they consider that after 1966 the Church adapted well to the American political context; and they believe that, while over-clericalized, the NCCB/USCC (United States Catholic Conference) complex has been an important media presence for the American Catholic community.

Fr. Reese has written what he saw, and what he sees reflects the insights not only of staff (e.g., Msgr. George G. Higgins) but of bishops like John Quinn, James Malone, and William McManus, those who at various stages played significant roles in key decisions of the American hierarchy. Of course, the official views are sifted through the author's own spectrum, which, if his earlier books *Archbishop* and *The Universal Catechism Reader* are true reflections, is less than favorable to Roman interventions in American Catholic affairs, whether it be to discipline an errant bishop or to write a catechism of the Catholic faith. Reese cites favorably the success of the first NCCB president (John F. Dearden) in implementing "the reforms of the Second Vatican Council and in guiding the bishops' Conferences to the role they currently play in the life of the Church". Especially important is his catalogue of the 119 major episcopal statements, half of which dealt with sociopolitical matters, and the reported successes NCCB leadership has had in developing consensus among bishops-in-the-field about the contemporary direction of the Church.

Like all commentaries of this kind, tidbits of information and/or political philosophy make interesting reading for the outsider, even if not fully explored by the insider. Such is Archbishop Daniel Pilarczyk's confession that the mood of the Conference is to choose a president "who is not going to be excessively creative". Or Bishop Malone's companionate observation that the bishop "who arrives in the president's chair has an entire agenda that is already in motion". Or Bishop Austin Vaughan's barb that the Conference presidents were neither "distinguished as ecclesiologists" nor "distinguished by their practice of collegiality". Very little in-depth analysis is given to the tension between Rome and the NCCB, although in one place (p. 265) Reese reports:

> The critical issues have been annulments, liturgy, and the bishops' control over theologians and religious educators. American culture also came under attack for its secularism, hedonism, individualism, and moral relativism. Vatican officials want the bishops to take a stronger hand with American theologians and be more critical of American culture.

Shepherds of the Flock is a process book. It describes the ecclesial game, inning by inning, but without an overall scorecard, without totalling the results at the "parish" level (that word does not appear in the index), largely because the umpires, relied upon for judgment, are drawn exclusively from the Washington Beltway. Assertions about "reforms" undertaken are numerous, but nowhere is information provided as to whether the Church is better than she was during National Catholic Welfare Conference (NCWC) days—in her worship and sacramental life, in her priesthood and religious life, in her teaching effectiveness, in her holiness.

However, it is precisely the relationship between process and results, between the Church's objectives and the state of Catholic affairs at the parish level, that determines whether the Church is on the right course and whether her management has been as effective as those of Fr. Reese's persuasion are inclined to believe.

The Beginnings of the NCCB

The National Conference of Catholic Bishops set out on a different course in the United States than its predecessor, the National Catholic Welfare Conference. NCWC was a World War I baby, a novelty, troublesome to Rome, and lacked a prepackaged design, except perhaps in its intention to provide services for widely scattered bishops in an ever-growing Church and, occasionally, to be a united voice for Catholic bishops in a country whose elites looked upon their ministrations with suspicion. The NCCB, and its counterpart on other continents, became something else—a conscious effort by an ecumenical council to decentralize a universal Church by balancing the primacy of the Pope with the collegiality of her bishops. Vatican II became the fulfillment of the early designs of Vatican I. Naturally, in the absence of guidelines from Rome on how this was to be done, local hierarchies enjoyed wide freedom to choose their own priorities, their own structures, and their own leaders. And, like the process which changed the Council itself from the original design of John XXIII, creating an

NCCB permitted some amply prepared bishops to assume the leading role, while others, certainly the majority, who were less well-prepared, generally remained passive during periods of change.

The year 1966 was a time in the nation's history when "privilege" was out and "commonality" in; when to be "hierarchy" was embarrassing, while being "democratic" was the only acceptable role; when ermine was out and wooden crosiers were in. A sign of the new mood appeared in evidence that year at the meeting which created the bishops' new conference. An obscure Bishop James Malone, not yet Ordinary of Youngstown, rose to suggest that the cardinals give up their seats of honor at all national meetings. (Interestingly, Cardinal Spellman did, but, true to form, Cardinal McIntyre held his ground, for a while at least.) Still, the sense of need to shift symbols of power within the hierarchy was already noticeable, and a new center for that power became inevitable.

The state of the Church then — in comparison with two years later — was still relatively calm. A major dispute over the morality of the anovulant pill was going on, but the Church's moral code was still intact among most Catholics. A bishop could still fire a troublesome theologian, as Rochester's James Kearney did when he sacked Charles Curran from St. Bernard's Seminary there. (The fact that he was nestled at the Catholic University without the by-your-leave of the rector, Bishop William McDonald, did not yet seem ominous.) Priests and religious were still entering Church service in large numbers and were clearly identifiable by their religious garb. Conversions to the Catholic faith continued to be high, well over one hundred thousand per annum. The Vincentian Fathers at St. John's University, with Joseph T. Cahill, C.M., in the lead, successfully withstood a strike of a faculty group, thereby keeping control of the university's Catholicity and moving on to become the largest Catholic university in the nation. Cardinal Shehan of Baltimore was preparing the first catechetical guidelines in the country to rein in his experimentalists in religious education, guidelines which included a condemnation of contraception. God was in his heaven, and the Barque of Peter was sailing in what looked like only a modest storm.

A fascinating aspect of the new power structure evolving in the post–Vatican II American Church was an unlikely progenitor, Edward Hoban, the archbishop-bishop (titular archbishop, bishop ordinary) of Cleveland. Hoban had been auxiliary to Chicago's triumphal George Cardinal Mundelein, and he was somewhat triumphal himself, but he possessed a large amount of charm and informality to boot. By virtue of the mysterious chemistry and circumstance that binds men to men, Hoban became a close personal friend of Archbishop Amleto Cicognani, apostolic delegate to the United States. Cicognani, appointed to his post by Pius XI, was out of favor with Pius XII, who had a unique relationship with Cardinal Spellman. While the New York Archbishop was considered a preeminent bishop-maker, Hoban contributed more to the post–Vatican II Church than Spellman. Four of his bishops—John Dearden (Detroit), John Krol (Philadelphia), John Whealon (Erie and Hartford), and Paul Hallinan (Charleston and Atlanta) —were to play major roles in the founding and early years of the NCCB. The first two were the initial president and vice president of the new NCCB, Hallinan was an important advisor to Dearden, while Whealon rose to become the bishop chosen to frame the *National Catechetical Directory.* Three would have been classified by reporters in 1966 as "conservatives", while Hallinan, a charming man, whose early prominence came as a campus minister on a secular campus and as a protégé of John Tracy Ellis, became a quintessential academic freedom-fighter for his friends in Catholic higher education.

After the Council, and by virtue of the disarray which ensued, the bishops of the United States became busier than their predecessors. Encouraged by the atmosphere of the times, they aspired to become listeners, and compassionate, more than authority figures or judges. By reason of the plethora of additional meetings they undertook to attend, bishops found themselves on the defensive in the face of challenges to their authority. They became aggressive fund-raisers too, not for the expansion of a growing Church, but to pay for the rising costs of operating shrinking institutions. Quite naturally, therefore, national episcopal affairs fell into the hands of peers who, busy themselves, had an aptitude for national politics. Only few had the vision and the will to organize the machinery that served their purposes.

Archbishop Dearden went into the Council known as "Iron John" for the way he ran the Diocese of Pittsburgh during his tenure there (1948–1959). Though he was not a canon lawyer, he was fundamentally a legalist who enforced the going law. When he thought there was a new charter, he proceeded according to character. The Council did not change Dearden as much as it changed his perspective. He was appointed to the Pontifical Birth Control Commission in the final days of its deliberations, chosen ostensibly to support Paul VI. Surprisingly, he ended up objecting to Paul VI's intervention in the Council on behalf of the doctrine taught by Pius XI and Pius XII and, eventually, voted with the majority of the Commission in favor of change. Dearden came home from Rome with new expectations of what the post–Vatican II Church was to be, and with new friends. There are bishops who insist he also came home anti-Roman. The Archbishop of Detroit was the chief architect of the NCCB and the dominant influence on its early decisions.

Thomas Reese indicated that the NCCB was structured to forestall the possibility of a Francis Cardinal Spellman ever again rising to dominate the American scene as that irrepressible New Yorker did in his lifetime. But Dearden may simply have been a prelate who, once in power, knew how to keep power close to him. Years later, John Cardinal Wright complained: "I'm no longer a member of the American hierarchy. Dearden says so!" Wright, Dearden's successor in Pittsburgh and cardinal prefect of the Congregation of the Clergy in Rome at the time, was annoyed.

He watched other curial cardinals go off to take part in and vote in the deliberations of their respective conferences. He himself did not. But Wright, with his learning, verbal skills, and Roman perspective, would surely have been a counterforce to Dearden's leadership. Detroit was not unmindful of that.

John Cardinal Krol was called a "conservative" by almost everyone, even Dearden's bureaucracy. A trained canon lawyer, he had a good sense of the Church. And his rise to prominence was somewhat phenomenal, reaching the cardinalate before Dearden, who was five years his senior. The story of that rise is worth telling. In 1954, Cardinal Spellman had arranged for his one-time auxiliary John O'Hara to succeed Cardinal Dougherty in Philadelphia. O'Hara's health failed in short order and, sensing an untimely end, the apostolic delegate polled the sitting archbishops for a candidate Rome might accept as O'Hara's successor. Bishop Krol, then in Cleveland, became the chosen candidate. But before Archbishop Vagnozzi could make the nomination, he discovered that Cardinal Spellman had once more beaten him to the draw. Krol, however, had the angels on his side, because Vagnozzi, by this time, had learned to work Spellman and was able to persuade the New York archbishop to withdraw his candidate. Krol, thereafter, not exactly the darling of the USCC bureaucracy, nonetheless became a team player, and when he succeeded to the presidency of the NCCB in 1971 (with St. Louis' John Cardinal Carberry as vice president), it became clear that the pre-set direction of the NCCB would stay on the course established by his predecessor. Indeed, Krol, who recognized the arrogance of academics when they crossed his path, could be very sharp in his dissection of their Achilles' heels. But he also took unkindly to criticism of the dysfunctions of ecclesial management, telling this or that Roman official, if need be, that he did not like to be lectured. Bristling at criticism was not a new episcopal response, but feeling frustrated about what to do with obvious wrongdoing became a commonplace reaction in Church headquarters almost everywhere.

The third figure of importance in the founding of the NCCB was Paul Hallinan, archbishop of Atlanta. In polite circles he was considered a "liberal", which he certainly thought himself to be. Like his mentor, he was caught up in the realm of ideas, perhaps because of his experience as a campus minister. While bishop of Charleston, he also went on to pursue a Ph.D. at Cleveland's Western Reserve University and became one of the Land O' Lakes original twenty-six cosigners (1967). This no doubt explains why, later in the year, he was the first episcopal member of the Catholic University Board of Bishops to favor retaining Charles Curran on faculty. As an apostle of institutional change, he also played an active role in the process by which that Board later capitulated to the young dissident.

Archbishop Dearden made him the first chairman of what was then called the NCCB's "Liturgical Apostolate". In this post, Hallinan set up the machinery and created the atmosphere under which the Latin liturgy became the English liturgy, tending to reinforce the mentality of those who, like CUA's Fr. Frederick McManus, were avid changemakers. Consistent with this ethos, anyone with a different view of what the Council had really said fell under his censure. Those of an earlier generation, who favored English in the liturgy long before Hallinan, would be hard-pressed to find in Council documents justification for some of the later liturgical upheavals in architecture, priestly practice, or even the translations, which no one at the time seriously scrutinized for unusual word changes. Bishops would find out only much later that the maxim *Lex orandi, lex credendi* deserved more attention than it received in 1966. The disappearance of the Latin liturgy itself was only one of the surprises, that liturgy which still inspires worldwide television audiences when celebrated in front of St. Peter's Basilica by John Paul II.

During that early postconciliar period, Archbishop Hallinan once wondered aloud "how we really worshipped God in any other way" than in English. He did not live long enough (d. 1967)

to experience the downslide in the modest Sunday Mass attendance in his small archdiocese. He also considered cautious
traditionalists, like Cardinal McIntyre, "absolutely stupid" in resisting
the vernacular. (McIntyre, hardly a theoretician of matters liturgical,
or even a good debater on the subject, was far from stupid, not
this man who turned Los Angeles into one of the major sees in the
country.) Hallinan even went out of his way to chide Washington's
Archbishop Patrick O'Boyle for his temerity in implementing
liturgical change. O'Boyle may have been the last prelate in the
Church to avoid doing what Church law required, but he was not
one to do anything without a plan.

Archbishop Hallinan made one other contribution to the bud-
ding NCCB. He sold Dearden on the value of Joseph Bernardin.
The latter, a priest of Charleston, was only a few years ordained
when Hallinan gave him high chancery-office status. Upon his
transfer to Atlanta, Hallinan persuaded Rome to give him an
auxiliary bishop in the person of Bernardin, who moved to Atlanta
in 1966. When, on Hallinan's death, Cardinal Spellman, dying
himself, sent a New York bishop to Atlanta, Bernardin was called
immediately to Washington, D.C., by Dearden, there to serve as
secretary general of the newly created United States Catholic
Conference. The rest is history.

Within the five-year term of Cardinal Dearden, the form and
shape of the National Conference of Catholic Bishops and its
chancery office—the USCC—were set. The specifics of the direction would soon become clear. The theological community, the
leadership of religious orders, and the presidents of major Catholic universities, mostly Jesuit at the time, were already seeking
autonomy from ecclesiastical supervision. In practice, this meant
preventing bishops from interfering with them in doing what
they decided to do on their own. In 1967, for example, Cardinal
Spellman opposed the Jesuits' decision to move Woodstock Seminary from Maryland to New York. The New Yorker had only
just died (December 2, 1967) when the Jesuits landed in Gotham

City, leaving the new archbishop unprepared for what became a scandal to faithful Jesuits and to Terence Cooke's people. This once-proud seminary died quickly, not least for the reason that two of its Jesuit progenitors left the priesthood. As the NCCB story began to unfold, the functions and dysfunctions of many new structures would appear on the ecclesial scene, sometimes simultaneously, depending on how well a sound or an unsound policy was executed.

There is a tendency among contemporary writers to overevaluate "men of ideas" in contradistinction to "the builders". Policies can be good or bad; executives responsible for sifting good ideas from bad may be effective in making sound policies work, or they may be incompetent. Bishops, for example, who approached changes in the liturgy with great care usually ended up with everything in place on time, with liturgical abuses held to the minimum. A story Archbishop Frank Furey of San Antonio often likes to tell illustrates the difference between "the dreamer" and "the builder". Rome called Furey from Philadelphia in 1966 to bail out the Diocese of San Diego, which was in serious financial difficulty, in large measure because of its obligation to the University of San Diego. Bishop Charles Buddy, that city's first ordinary (1936), had been the prime mover in bringing this diocesan college into existence (1949). To save both the Diocese and the University, Furey turned to Cardinal McIntyre of Los Angeles, whose business acumen and contacts were widely respected. McIntyre assembled the money package which insured the survival of both institutions. As Furey told the story: "I thanked the Cardinal, whose only response was, 'Think nothing of it, Frank; but remember that forty years down the road, no one will ever know either of us was here. They'll only say what a man of great vision Bishop Buddy was!' "

The NCCB Response to Battle

That war is hell was understood by rational mankind long before the American Civil War. That battles are cruel and inhuman punishment inflicted on the innocent as well as the guilty was appreciated long before the Battle of Jericho. Although the words "war" and "battle" appear approximately 396 times in the Old and New Testaments, starting with the good angels against the bad, St. Ambrose (at least until he was contradicted by the invasion of Rome by Attila the Hun) was naïve enough to think that a new *Pax Romana Catholica* was possible in his time, with Christian bishops in their cathedrals and a Christian sitting in the Imperial Seat. It required a more realistic St. Augustine to define why just wars are needed—not for aggression on other peoples' rights or properties—but to defend *Domus, Patria, Corpus Christi* from unfriendly threats to their existence. Naturally, there had to be a good chance of winning the battle or the war, but this required prudent judgment, and ecclesiastical superiors, as much as civil emperors, were expected to be prudent men.

That an ecclesial war has been going on within the Catholic Church has been obvious since 1960, shortly after John XXIII announced the coming of Vatican II. The declaration of war in the United States came immediately after the Council, made by Charles Curran on behalf of theologians, by Theodore Hesburgh on behalf of college presidents, and by Jesuits on behalf of religious communities. Thirty years later, theologians unashamedly tell bishops they will accept no mandate from the hierarchy to teach faith and morals, even though in civil society practitioners of certain scientific arts require licenses from competent authority even to build bridges. John Paul II has tried valiantly to bring Jesuits back under the jurisdiction of the pope, but these religious continue to be the leading *antimagisterial* force within the Church. The three substructures mentioned manage a large portion of the diocesan and parochial machinery through which bishops are expected to make disciples.

A review of the way in which this war has been conducted from 1965 to this day may be helpful in determining how it can be brought to a happy conclusion. Even if not every theologian, every college president, or every religious superior will be happy with the proper results. It may be noticed during this review that the aggressors against the *magisterium* are armed with new defense mechanisms (the primacy of rights over duties, of the individual over the common good; new rhetoric stressing politics and power as critical issues, not Catholic truth), and with new weapons (threats, strikes, plebiscites, and polls). Counteraction by the *magisterium,* the antagonists made clear, was to take place in dialogue, not through the use of *magisterial* force.

Deciding which event or circumstance became our ecclesiastical Pearl Harbor is not easy. We can start almost anywhere. The following arrangement is arbitrary but not necessarily mindless:

The Curran Debacle. Friends of Curran still say the issue was birth control. A larger perspective indicates that Catholic truth in a major doctrinal teaching was the issue, along with the obligation of bishops to protect this truth. Quarantining those who threatened the Church's survival in the life of Catholics was only one option. The CUA Board of Bishops, at first, had the right idea (1967) in denying Curran a new contract. But some bishops, aided by Washington academics, talked other bishops into capitulating. The Church would look bad before the American public, they said, if bishops interfered with academic freedom. (The majority of bishops to this day accept this policy, even though everyone interferes with academic freedom, and not least of all today's academics, once in power.) Not even the redoubtable Archbishop O'Boyle could explain satisfactorily why "We had to eat crow", except to say that he was outvoted. Curran, now a tenured CUA professor, went on to create havoc the following year (1968) by leading a frontal assault on *Humanae vitae.* Only O'Boyle had the courage to face up to the confrontation. Then, as

if to pour salt into the ecclesial wounds, the NCCB, in defending
Humanae vitae with a pastoral of their own (1968), established
"norms of licit theological dissent" (Curran in the wings, con-
senting), which in practice, as far as the theological community
was concerned, became "the right of public dissent". Years later,
Cardinal Hickey and Cardinal Ratzinger in Rome would disavow
the existence of any such right, but by then the damage was done.
The bishops fired Curran at Rome's request—nineteen years after
the initial rebellion. But by 1986 Catholic opinion on contraception,
and on many other Catholic doctrines, had gone the way of
Curran and his academic allies. Between 1967 and 1986, Curran
had risen to be head of CUA's theology department, in which he
controlled appointments, pay raises, and tenure. It should surprise
few that the Currans of this world regularly do what they said
bishops should not do, that is, fashion a university department
their way.

Of course, the Curran debacle did more than injure the status
of the hierarchy. It raised questions about the truth of the Church's
moral demands, confounded the nature of Catholic theology, and
gave power (independent of Church supervision) to an academic
establishment which never before, in the United States at least,
had claimed or had been allowed to usurp such autonomous
control over the lives of the faithful. Catholic theology, today as
always, remains a "science" only in the widest possible sense. Its
truth is not determined by academic research, however much
detailed study helps explicate its meaning. College professors do
not determine doctrine, nor do they finalize ecclesial policies
based on that doctrine. However, the permissiveness implicit in
unrestrained dissent, whether in family or in social institutions
(e.g., religious orders), usually begets arrogance in the practitioners and spawns a variety of antisocial or antiecclesial types,
hardly consonant with gospel holiness.

Immediately after Curran's victory, the entire mood on Catholic campuses, almost everywhere, became *antimagisterial*. The only restraints placed on anyone were those put on the defenders of Catholic teaching. Jesuit theologians John Ford, John Lynch, and Joseph Farraher went into veritable exile. The staff of *America* was emptied of loyalists almost overnight. Msgr. Eugene Kevane, head of the School of Education prior to the strike at CUA, lost his post because he had insisted on holding classes during the strike. Fr. Manuel Miguens, who had better academic credentials in theology and biblical studies than Raymond Brown, was later denied tenure at CUA because he had criticized Brown.

One of the least-told stories of 1967 is how Apostolic Delegate Vagnozzi, sensing the changed mood of the Administrative Board toward Curran, and surely not without touching base with Rome, asked Cardinal Spellman (then in the last six months of his life) to persuade the Board to close down CUA for the summer session. (Spring classes were already at an end.) Let Curran picket an empty campus, he suggested. About the same time, Fr. John McMahon, S.J., one-time provincial, and Fr. Robert Gannon, S.J., retired president of Fordham University, also sought the intervention of the old Cardinal against what was then going on within Jesuit circles to the harm of the Church. Spellman's response to both requests was similar: "I've been in battles all my life; I'm too old for another one. Whatever the bishops decide is all right with me."

Of course, the politicking was also intense. Msgr. Joseph N. Moody, a New York priest teaching Church history at CUA, traveled to his native city for a visit with his classmate John Maguire, Spellman's co-adjutor archbishop. Moody, a delegate of one, wanted Maguire to use his influence to keep Spellman out of personal involvement in the Curran brouhaha. Maguire, at least, would have reported the Moody visit to the Cardinal. It was the end of an era, with little promise of better things to come.

Religious Superiors: Their Colleges and Convents. The "year of conspiracy" might be a good lead-in for a Church manual dealing with 1967: April 10th, a critical day for Charles Curran; July 23rd, the revolt of college presidents at Land O' Lakes, Wisconsin; October 14th, when the Immaculate Heart of Mary Sisters in Los Angeles threw down the gauntlet by refusing to accept Rome's definition of the "essential elements" for religious life.

The NCCB did nothing about any of the three rebellions. Later its bishop presidents would side with the college presidents against Rome. As late as 1982, the soon-to-be president of the NCCB, Bishop James Malone, personally led a delegation to John Paul II to plead against any Roman intervention in American Catholic higher education. The anti-Roman passions of years gone by were as alive as they had been in 1972, when Theodore Hesburgh, C.S.C., and Robert Henle, S.J., stood up in Rome at an international meeting of college presidents (IFCU) to warn Gabriel Cardinal Garrone: Hesburgh to say that, if Rome insisted upon its norms prevailing, he would lead the American delegation out of the meeting; Henle to threaten he would have Georgetown University abandon its Catholic identity. Now, twenty-odd years later, when John Paul II demands "ordinances" of some kind to insure the integrity of the Catholicity such institutions claim for themselves, the Jesuit presidents inform the American bishops (December 1, 1993) that their institutions cannot make an act of Catholic faith. As if they themselves cannot or as if they will not assemble boards which will. As if the presidents of Harvard and Yale do not make an act of faith in their belief system, which they continue to impose on Cambridge and New Haven.

When Cardinal J. Francis A. McIntyre insisted to IHMs that only those religious who accepted the "essential elements" of religious life were eligible for assignments in the Los Angeles Catholic schools, he found himself standing alone, abandoned by the California bishops. Thus began the demise of the greatest instrument of evangelization the universal Church had ever seen, i.e., the American parochial school system. Five years later, the Conference of Major Superiors of Women, a Roman creation to provide unity in the voice of religious women, became the Leadership Conference of Women Religious, without so much as a by-your-leave to the NCCB and as if to say to Rome, "No more Superiors anywhere." But, lest anyone think that only anti-Roman forces were coddling disobedient religious, it should be mentioned that bishops considered "conservative" by *Commonweal* (e.g., John Cardinal Cody of Chicago and Milwaukee Archbishop William Cousins) were also telling Rome to stay out of the "religious" fight, lest the nuns abandon their schools. They departed anyway, and the LCWR, its revolution accomplished, is itself dying today.

When the chapter in *The Battle for the American Church* entitled "Embattled Nuns" was in draft form, it was sent to the apostolic delegate in Washington, D.C., for review—to make sure that it was error-free and that the case was not overstated. The response of the late Thomas Gallagher, O.P., who was interlocutor for the delegation on matters pertaining to religious, replied: "Don't change a word! Do you need any further information?"

The NCCB–USCC Aftermath. By the end of the first five-year term of Cardinal Dearden (1965–1971), the ethos and direction of the American Church's immediate future was set to favor the Washington, D.C., bureaucracies at the Catholic University of America, the Jesuit Conference, the National Catholic Educational Association, the Association of Catholic Colleges and Universities, the Conference of Major Superiors of Men, and the Leadership Conference of Women Religious. Clearly out of influence in the Catholic Beltway, not only out but resented, were such groups as Opus Dei and Catholics United for the Faith.

While advocating the "open Church" everywhere else in the Church, the Washington apparatus retained close control of the national episcopal agenda. Dearden himself knew how to hold executive sessions of bishops within his preferred bounds. Even the power of appointing staff to the USCC was vested in the general secretary, a man always beholden to the NCCB president, as Bishop James Rausch discovered, he who ended up as bishop of

Phoenix, when he stepped out of the subservient role of general secretary to the NCCB president, then Joseph Bernardin. One archbishop, noticing how Dearden tended to close off discussion once he got two or three bishops to favor something that interested him, threatened to seize the microphone if passed over again. He won the right to object. A cardinal complained how one of his suffragans found his committee oversupplied with feminists, but when he wished to add a nationally known antifeminist, the general secretary told him that the lady in question was unacceptable to his USCC staff. Another cardinal related that a new bishop was dissatisfied with the make-up of a committee, whose chairman he now was, only to be told by another general secretary, "You bishops have to learn that you're not running this place." More recently, a zealous ordinary, elected to the chairmanship of an important NCCB committee, where an executive secretary was also needed, was advised by a bishop friend to choose his "exec" carefully because the aide would be the day-to-day manager of the committee. To this suggestion the new chairman responded, as if in surprise, "But that appointment is made, not by me, but by the USCC general secretary." In the end, the bishop-chairman, persuaded otherwise, did succeed in choosing his own "exec".

The most notorious exercise of centralized power against bishops-in-the-field was the appointment in 1986 of Michael J. Buckley, S.J., as executive secretary of the NCCB Committee on Doctrine. When the name first surfaced in public, the initial objections to giving such a role to Buckley came from fellow Jesuits. They did not think he was a strong defender of the faith in the John Paul II mold. Bishop Austin Vaughan's *obiter dicta* at an NCCB meeting came to their mind: "It's a case of the fox guarding the henhouse!" At the ensuing episcopal meeting in Collegeville (1986), two cardinals objected, and the name was withdrawn. No sooner had the bishops returned to their dioceses than San Francisco's Archbishop John Quinn, one-time president of the NCCB and Buckley's sponsor, counter-objected. A reevaluation was made by a committee, appointed by the NCCB president and headed by Archbishop Pilarczyk (a future president). The charges made against Buckley by the cardinals were rejected by Pilarczyk. The Jesuit was reappointed for five years. He left that post in 1991 to become a theology professor for Richard McBrien at Notre Dame.

Thomas Reese's *Shepherds of the Flock* accepts the developments within the NCCB as quite normal, consistent with Vatican II goals, and representative of the American episcopal mind. Unquestionably, the Dearden-Bernardin leadership of the NCCB in the first five years (1966–1971) set the American Church on this course, one which did not derive purely from Council documents. After Dearden, and during Krol's presidency (1971–1974), Bernardin retained control of the national machinery. This one-time general secretary succeeded Krol, and his leadership style, which he later credited to Dearden and Hallinan, continued the course set in 1966. It has not been challenged to this day, even though not a few bishops and cardinals are dissatisfied. One archbishop claims Dearden would never have been given a five-year term if "we had known what he was like"! Another veteran archbishop wrote: "There was more freedom at the national level when Spellman and Stritch ran things!" Many bishops do not actively participate in national affairs because they feel it is a waste of time. One archbishop, going home after the debacle of the "women's pastoral", reported: "Just left another disaster!" However, bishops satisfied with the Bernardin system, especially those who were terribly upset by Rome's putative effort to depose Hunthausen, take in stride the bushels of documents shipped to them two weeks before a national meeting, leaving them little time to digest proposals, to decide whether they might help or harm the Church, little time to think how critical questions should be debated, let alone answered.

A peculiar mind-set can be found in the bishops who see only good in the NCCB's present course. One archbishop friendly to "the Club" asked a few years ago why a certain priest, with a decent theological reputation, hated the Church. The prelate really did not know the man in question, and the priest had never directed any criticism at this particular bishop. The archbishop knew only that he was dealing with a public critic of general absolution, bad catechetics, loosely given *imprimaturs,* and liturgical abuses in diocesan seminaries, criticisms which some of the bishop's own priests were leveling against him. But that kind of convoluted thinking about the correct ecclesial order was commonplace during the 1970s. The cards had already been stacked in high places against the so-called orthodox point of view. Jesuits were in, Opus Dei was out; Sr. Francis Borgia of the Leadership Conference was in, Mother Claudia of the Consortium was out; Theodore Hesburgh, C.S.C., of Notre Dame was in, Joseph T. Cahill, C.M., of St. John's University was out; Richard McCormick was in, Germain Grisez was out; Msgr. Frederick McManus and the Canon Law Society were in, Ralph McInerny and the Fellowship of Catholic Scholars were out; *America* magazine was in, while *Homiletic and Pastoral Review* was out; and so forth.

The Charted Course. Before he left office, Dearden authorized four "scientific" studies of the priesthood, under the aegis of six priests chosen by his aides: two theologians, two sociologists, one psychologist, and one Church historian. To any informed person, the six editors were anti-Church authority. Four of these priest-authors eventually left the priesthood, and the theological study itself, based on biblical theories like Raymond Brown's, was formally rejected by the bishops. (But it was published anyway.) All four studies, however, were highly critical of a very successful institutional Church. Even the commissioned history of the American priesthood expended its scholarship on the internal fights of clerics, and, in an index covering six hundred pages and one thousand footnotes, the words "pastor", "parish priest", and "parochial" were nowhere to be found. An earlier Church historian might have given major credit to parish priests for the creation of one of the finest parish systems the Christian world has ever seen, but a reader of this book would never know a thing about that. (Most of the contributors to this NCCB book, including its editor, lacked any experience in building or maintaining a parish church.) Cardinal Krol, once he succeeded to the NCCB presidency in 1971, was asked to quash the four studies before they could do harm to the Church, but the archbishop of Philadelphia confessed that his involvements within his own archdiocese precluded him from doing that.

Then, "experiments" began—which were not experiments at all; new procedures for marriage tribunals, Holy Communion first for eight year olds, with Confession coming later, and liturgical novelties which allowed recalcitrant changemakers (wrongly) to legitimize Mass without vestments, to alter or omit sections of the Mass, like the Nicene Creed or Eucharistic Prayers, or to substitute Daniel Berrigan or *Time* magazine for Peter, James, and John. So easily did abuses slip into the Catholic way of parochial service that by 1967 an obscure but well-intentioned priest advised his peers that the old Catholic virtues were of little value in the post–Vatican II Church.[1] Another serious but unappreciated dysfunction from those early days was the rush to retire pastors forcibly, to limit a pastor's term of office to twelve years, and to turn young priests unqualified for the title into "associate" pastors overnight. Not only was the era of legendary pastors over (time is needed for legends to be created), but the priesthood became another job without deference, reverence, or obedience.

Suddenly, a spate of pastorals on worldly concerns arrived on the scene, also sorties against Roman efforts to protect sound teaching and catechesis, and more studies. The Church's priorities were being reordered, and very few seemed to mind. Ten years ago or more, J. Brian Benestad's *The Pursuit of a Just Social Order* compared the policy statements of the bishops (1966–1980) with the overall thrust of Catholic social teaching going on back to Leo XIII and Pius X. The newer teaching from the Church's Washing-

---

[1] *Homiletic and Pastoral Review,* August 1967.

ton headquarters, he discovered, when compared with episcopal statements prior to 1962, failed to confront the issues posed by the country's secular establishment. Said Benestad: "The bishops have unwittingly allowed the secular world to set their political agenda." Whereas the NCWC statements were concerned with character formation and unjust personal behavior, the post–Vatican II episcopal statements were preoccupied with structural changes in society, usually in a manner which disturbed the secular status quo hardly at all.

On critical questions touching upon the faith or its transmission, the bishops' staff were not at all shy about challenging the Catholic status quo. The specter of a USCC staff, led by Msgr. William McManus, leading a fight in Rome (1971) against a *General Catechetical Directory* or, as a bishop, standing up at a November 1977 meeting to demand that the episcopal body reject amendments to the proposed *National Catechetical Directory* (dealing with content) because "they were unacceptable to staff" surely provided a case study of how carts can be invented to pull horses. Bishop James Rausch, USCC successor to Bernardin as general secretary, today is cited (by Thomas Reese) as responsible for the 1975 debacle in Detroit named "Call to Action" (on behalf of a less doctrinal, more humanistic Church); but he may have done more harm when he came before a group of university professors at CUA to demean his seminary education, an important segment of which took place in Rome.

The story of episcopal involvement in undermining its own traditional mission unfolded with imperfect guidelines for sexuality, in wrongheaded first drafts of pastorals, when reports rejected by bishops as unsatisfactory were published anyway (e.g., on AIDS), and in one-sided consultations stacked against authentic teaching, as in the peace and women's pastorals, both of which evoked major Roman interventions. In one case a relatively unknown auxiliary bishop was chosen as a reputed hawk for a "peace committee" that included four doves, led by Archbishop Bernardin.

Not only did the young bishop find himself out-voted 4 to 1 by the bishops, but by 9 to 1 when the five staff members of the USCC were present. With the help of Cardinal Ratzinger, John J. O'Connor survived that one, but many bishops have told a similar tale about how they found themselves invited into a machinery whose agenda was prepackaged.

If skewed performances by the NCCB/USCC bureaucracy are addressed publicly, unwanted criticism results for those who notice, and sometimes an unfriendly reaction from bishops at a national meeting. But many bishops are frustrated by what they see. When the ill-dated 1987 AIDS document, which approved the dissemination of factual information to students about condoms, was buried a year later, Bishop Eusebius J. Beltran, then of Tulsa, now of Oklahoma City, rose at the June 24–27, 1988, meeting in Collegeville, to object to such statements becoming known as "statements of the body of bishops":

> I suggest that the body of bishops should use this unfortunate episode as the occasion to reconsider very carefully the policies, practices and procedures involved in the issuance of documents by the NCCB and USCC. At times there seems to be an almost frantic urgency in those organizations to issue statements, testimony, policy papers, pastoral letters, and the like.

Perhaps the greatest affront to ecclesial decency was the response by the NCCB in 1977 to Fr. Joseph T. Cahill, C.M. Cardinal Gabriel Garrone had suggested to Cahill that he bring a different view of the Catholicity of the Church's higher education to American bishops from the one articulated frequently by Notre Dame's Theodore Hesburgh. Cardinal Terence Cooke arranged his meeting in Cincinnati with the then NCCB president, Joseph Bernardin. The Archbishop was gracious, making a few complaints of his own, one being that Rome was pushing him to do something about Charles Curran, whom he called a "heretic". This demand, he said complainingly, his predecessor (Cardinal

Krol) refused to touch. Bernardin accepted Fr. Cahill's written request for episcopal help to universities hoping to stay Catholic and promised to get back to the SJU president with a formal response. This he did not do. The subject, however, was placed on the agenda of the next meeting of the NCCB Administrative Board, but the presentation was made, not by Fr. Cahill, but by Fr. Hesburgh, who simply asked the bishops to "Trust us." Not a single bishop asked any of the questions Cardinal Garrone wanted answered by the bishops.

Later in the same year the Fellowship of Catholic Scholars came into being as a response to Cardinal Garrone's question: "Is there no other voice within American Catholic higher education than that of the NCEA and Fr. Hesburgh?" Fr. Ronald Lawler, O.F.M. Cap., the first president, paid a courtesy call on Bishop Thomas Kelly. He found the USCC general secretary courteous but distracted and seemingly disinterested. Two years later, when James Hitchcock, the second president, led a delegation to the NCCB president, Archbishop John Quinn, he encountered studied indifference, if not veiled hostility.

By this time practically everyone knew the Church was in trouble. So, at Rome's urging, "studies" of religious communities and seminaries were undertaken. (Interestingly, no one at that time pursued Garrone's interest in what was going on within the Catholic halls of ivy.) Bishop John Marshall (Burlington) began the analysis with high hopes but in due course was persuaded to include on his visiting committees the very kinds of seminary people that were creating the formation problems under review. A seminary, like a medical school for doctors, after all, is to train functioning priests, not psychedelic debaters or abstract researchers. In one visit to Dunwoodie Seminary, for example, leading committee members (a bishop included) were critical of the clerical attire worn by the student body and the plethora of papal encyclicals available in the book store. Later still, Rome would intervene to chide the Washington Theological Union for its defective training of future religious priests, not only about its dubious notions of the priesthood, but even about its inadequate Catholic ecclesiology. Today, in many such places, formation is more psychological than spiritual. Rules are few. Theology is often taught open-endedly. And orientation courses, sometimes led by women who might profit from reorientation in the essential elements of religious life, strive to make future priests sensitive to feminists.

When, during Rome's study of religious communities, Archbishop John Quinn indicated that all was going reasonably well in religious life in spite of particular difficulties, a theologian whose mission, week by week, was to give retreats to religious communities across the country wrote to inquire whether the Archbishop and he lived on the same planet. Churchgoers, who saw religious communities collapsing all around them, would have agreed with the theologian, not with Quinn.

By 1984 the charted course of the NCCB leadership was set as much for bishops-in-the-field as for the Church as a whole. The new Code of Canon Law was in place (1983), but important segments of its demands were already unenforced letters in the United States. John Paul II was traveling all over the world speaking of bad theology and showing particular interest in episcopal conferences and their adherence to universal norms; academics were defending people like Edward Schillebeeckx and liberation theologians, once they came under fire in Rome; the Pope had called for an extraordinary synod of bishops, even as the Catholic Press Association criticized the Vatican's insistence that *imprimaturs* be withdrawn from certain catechisms; and the Notre Dame Study of American Parish Life, put together by two afficionados of the United States Catholic Conference, made it very clear that "pick and choose Catholicism" was not only alive and well but quite proper for American Catholics to follow; religious orders were again under scrutiny at Rome's insistence, and John Paul II began to annoy moral theologians more than ever by insisting, on July 18, 1984, to be exact, that the contraceptive norm proclaimed by Paul VI, as well as by Pius XI earlier, "belongs not only to the natural law but also to the moral order revealed by God".

Any journalist observing this scenario might have concluded that the "so-called liberal agenda", promoted so vigorously by the Church's reforming party, was on the wrong track, if only because the Pope seemed to be going in a different direction. Indeed, many journalists were saying so, and a goodly number of reformers, too, insisted that Rome was trying to undo Vatican II. But within the NCCB, that same July 1984, an unsigned report was passed around entitled "Recent Activism by Conservative Catholics in the United States", whose insights (the report said, p. 2) were based on "file material from the Nunciature and the Episcopal Conference".

The tone of the report is temperate, but it concentrates, not on the forces directed against the Pope's clear agenda, but on conservatives who were directing complaints about the American Catholic situation "not just to, but against bishops, both individually and collectively". The report explains, however, in a matter-of-fact way, the reason for giving particular attention at that time to conservative activists. Groups such as Catholics United for the Faith and the Fellowship of Catholic Scholars and publishers of the *Homiletic and Pastoral Review* and *Catholics in Crisis* (now *Crisis*) were such activists, as were sundry local groups which, "in their various ways, are the guardians and defenders of traditional Catholic values in the face of deviations by bishops, their clerical and lay collaborators, and official Church offices, institutions, and organizations". The reason given for the report's exclusive concern with conservatives was: "[While liberal pressure groups are still around] the liberal agenda of the 1960's and 1970's has either been achieved or is now viewed by its advocates as achievable in a longer time frame than originally envisaged." The report continues: "Yesterday's liberal activists have become members of today's Catholic establishment."

This unpublished report made its way to Rome, where perhaps it was intended to go, but it could not have originated with an obscure bureaucrat, even though a second-level official, with access to Bishop James Malone's files (he was NCCB president at the time) and those of Archbishop Pio Laghi, was clearly the redactor. John Paul II may have been focusing on internal Church division over Catholic truth as distinguished from error, on moral right as different from moral wrong; but from the paper's title onward, the report interpreted the Catholic crisis in purely political terms—"liberals" vs. "conservatives". And, although the author concedes that the conservatives might be right sometimes, they are, in his view, the ones who must be somehow "dialogued" into "the mainstream of Catholic organizational and institutional life". On the issue of orthodoxy, "the presumption must be in favor of the bishops both individually and collectively." The report never defines "orthodoxy", nor how it relates to warring segments of the Church. Those who would conserve worship, faith, and morals as John Paul II insisted are lumped together as conservatives with those within the Church whose prudential judgments favored the socioeconomic policies of a Barry Goldwater over those of a Lyndon Baines Johnson. Those two groups, radically different ideologically, and distinct in their relations with the hierarchy, were hardly conservative in the same way.

What outsiders might not readily grasp is that, by 1984, "power politics", i.e., prevailing force, had become as much-used a tool in doctrinal debates as it was in conflicts between nations. The language of Hans Küng, Andrew Greeley, and Richard McBrien was studded with concepts like "power to the people" or to the academic class. Less noticed perhaps were the subtle assertions of someone like Raymond Brown (especially in his *Community of the Beloved Disciple,* 1979), where he freely associates orthodox belief with what "prevailed" in the Church (e.g., Irenaeus over the Gnostics) or what "won out" (like Athanasius over Arius).

In any event, the anonymous author of "Recent Activism by

Conservative Catholics in the United States" had one thing right: doctrinal conservatives, even those fully committed to the thrust of Vatican II, were outside the Washington, D.C., episcopal machinery by 1984, no matter how inside they might have been with individual bishops and/or with Roman cardinals. Some diocesan bishops knew this, others preferred not to notice, many went along with the leadership in power, that leadership which, following its charted course, deeply resented—and labeled pejoratively—those who, not unlike John Paul II, challenged the direction the Conference had taken since 1966. One only need note, as many bishops did, the featured stars of *Origins* year after year or the ideology of those regularly invited to instruct or advise bishops at their national meetings. One rarely saw the names of Germain Grisez, John Finnis, William May, Ralph McInerny, Janet Smith, Joyce Little, or their like. The die had been cast a long time before, and the argument now in process is whether it was cast by the right hands.

The 1993 NCCB Board Meetings. As the years have passed, more and more bishops complain, by and large privately, about the conduct of their national machinery. The mistranslation of the universal catechism (with doctrinal implications) brought Cardinal Ratzinger into the fray, making all translations of psalms, prayers, and liturgical texts suspect in some minds. The suggestion was widespread that changes in praying could signify changes in Church teaching. Translations, therefore, became a hot topic at the 1993 meeting. When the Grail translation of the Psalms came up for a vote of approval, the headlines read "Bishops Reject Grail Translation", which was not exactly true. The vote was 150 for, only 98 against, but short of the two-thirds necessary to send it to Rome for final approval. A substantial majority, therefore, were inclined to trust what their leadership offered.

The minutes of the September 1993 Administrative Board/ Committee Meetings also indicate that a large amount of time is still spent on staff research papers, on subjects like the North

American Free Trade Agreement or the predilections of the National Advisory Council, or in trying to distinguish who gave what money to the Holy See. The most important Catholic issue facing the bishops well into the twenty-first century is what Catholic higher education is doing to advance or detract from the holiness of the faithful and their family life. This subject matter was dismissed in *just seven lines,* with the promise of further discussion in 1994.

The weight of national decision-making still belongs with the top episcopal machinery. Mother Angelica finds herself in trouble with the NCCB president for making a public complaint that the Church was not served well at World Youth Day when, during the Stations of the Cross, a woman (not a man) was chosen to mime Christ. The assembled bishops are told, in defense, that the mistake was merely the result of a comedy of errors. No one on the staff of the USCC, which ran the event, was chided as Mother Angelica was, and no bishop rose to request a better explanation of a strange occurrence having more than artistic implications. Cardinal Hickey, who fought in Rome and finally won canonical status for the Council of Major Superiors of Women Religious, was also forced to remind the NCCB leadership that this new group of major superiors was to be consulted on all matters of religious life, not ignored as they had been recently by the staff. Support for the righteous was still hard to come by within USCC precincts.

Origins is another example of business as usual in the Beltway. As a documentary service, it provides its readership with the official records of the Church, from episcopal decrees to Roman pastorals. But, like *Herder's Correspondence* during the Council, its editors face a wide variety of choices among the interpreters and reinterpreters of those documents. And they regularly publish spokesmen closely associated with the Catholic associations in and around the United States Catholic Conference. Rarely do they solicit or publish, preferentially at least, the many lectures or position papers critical of the dissenting establishment or of the present state of Catholic affairs. In 1993, for example, two hundred bishops assembled in Dallas to discuss Catholic family life and the modern difficulties pertaining thereto. One panel of three clerics featured two positive assessments of the teaching in *Humanae vitae,* and the third address was given by Avery Dulles, who suggested that *Humanae vitae* should not be a *litmus test* for choosing bishops. The Dulles remarks were widely featured in the Catholic press, prompting the editor of *Origins* to seek permission to reprint his entire text. *Origins* received permission, but only on condition that all three talks of those panelists be published simultaneously. The predilection of that editor for Dulles alone demonstrated anew, as if it were necessary, that the more things change in Rome, the more they remain the same at the USCC.

Chapter Five

National Episcopal Conferences and Rome

Not many years ago, an aide to a prefect of a major Roman congregation walked into the office of his boss with folders of complaints against four American bishops. The younger man, placing the material on the cardinal's desk, said: "Your Eminence, the Pope has to fire these four bishops." To which the older man replied: "As usual, you have it all wrong. The Pope doesn't have to fire four bishops. He only has to fire one, and tell the world why he fired him."

This little interplay between two friends, whatever else it may signify, reinforces the notion that, in the final analysis, the well-being of the Catholic community is in the hands of the Church's pastors. This may explain why history books are filled with the doings of bishops more than the good works of saints. In the cited case, the cardinal told his junior that the function of the Church's hierarchy, as part of their witness to the Church's faith, is to restrain serious reported evildoing, even if the perpetrators are themselves part of the hierarchy.

Observers of the Catholic scene who believe that what the Church teaches is true also have a good recollection of what Rome has been saying for years about the American Church. And about what John Paul II has indicated are his problems with certain American bishops. Some of these commentators may report the papal criticisms crudely, even bitterly, but their bad form does not invalidate the Pope's case, which can be made sincerely, forcibly, but in good taste:

1. We now have disobedient bishops in the United States, some of whose strange opinions or behavior have doctrinal ramifications.

2. We now have a divided hierarchy, evident in the conduct of the National Conference of Catholic Bishops, a situation which the Holy See thus far has been unable to rectify.

3. The lack of unity and discipline is even more widespread in the Church's infrastructures and in a wide variety of diocesan parishes.

4. While the disobedient elements within the Catholic community remain unhappy with the Pope, because their errant beliefs and conduct have failed to acquire official sanction, it is the obedient bishops, priests, and laity who suffer under scandals, bad teaching, and sometimes from media displeasure, simply because they are witnesses to authentic Catholicity or object to the undisciplined and uncertain state of the Church.

It is one thing, for example, for a dissenter or a quasi-heretic to shunt faithful Catholics or a good cause to the fringes of the Church; quite another when a bishop does the same, claiming for himself the role of "moderate". One notorious incident of this kind occurred when Newark's Archbishop Peter Gerety, ordered by Rome to withdraw the *imprimatur* from Anthony Wilhelm's *Christ among Us* for reasons of doctrinal insufficiency and aberrations, made this comment about the effect of his announcement: "[It] created quite a stir, since the only people who complained about the book in this country, as far as I know, are the extreme right-wing groups who have been giving some of the bishops so much trouble in other areas also."[1] So much also for Rome's competence in discerning doctrinal error.

[1] *Origins,* March 7, 1985, p. 621.

Gerety obviously did not believe the substance of Ratzinger's criticism.

These human failings of the Church are never going to be remedied by majority vote, or by dialogue, or by patient suffering, although suffering joined to Christ's has redemptive value into eternity. And, because the government of the Church is not tripartite, the buck of responsibility falls on the shoulders of bishops in union with the Pope to deal with bishops not in union with the Pope. The principle of subsidiarity applies here, of course. Fraternal correction at the local levels, preferable in executive session, is a starting point, although a rarity. Special responsibility falls on archbishops, who have larger canonical roles, and on cardinals, who are personal advisors to the Pope on a wide range of matters. Their personal influence is not so noticeable on the centralized bureaucracy as once it was. Still, apostolic constitutions, canon law or papal decrees, properly promulgated to be enforced uniformly, are needed to maintain decent and consistent ecclesial order across the universal Church. The faith and moral life of the faithful demand no less. Even evangelization becomes only a pious wish whenever the Church's trumpet sounds not only uncertain but cacophonous. No one who loves the Church wishes to see bishops brawling in public. But, for over twenty-five years, individual bishops have been known to make inexact or incorrect doctrinal statements, give diocesan favor to known dissidents, and indicate their disagreement with Roman policies, even with its supervision. Some of these have had unusual influence on the conduct of ecclesial structures within the Washington Beltway. And they remain uncorrected.

The Holy See has recognized these episcopal problems from the very beginning, has spoken loudly and often about them, but its stick then, as now, seems to be made of balsa wood. As one critical issue rose after the other, the Pope's Curia moved carefully to set limits on the scope of the doctrinal playing field. Cardinal Cicognani was very clear on the immutability of the Church's teaching on contraception. Cardinal Garrone was forthright about limits on the autonomy of Catholic colleges. Cardinal Wright minced no words about the mess in catechetics. Cardinal Hamer, with Archbishop Meyer, was quite specific about what was wrong with the way religious communities were going. And, yet, abuses in all four areas continued to accumulate, abetted by local prelates, until it was difficult to know anymore what was authentically Catholic about long-established Church infrastructures.

Individual American bishops are not the only offenders. In 1992 in Regensberg, Germany, two cardinals duelled in public over birth control, the older of the two not at all sympathetic with the *magisterium.* Toward the end of 1993, three German bishops, for the most part protégés of Cardinal Ratzinger, issued a pastoral, on their own initiative and independently of the German conference, which told divorced and civilly remarried German Catholics they might receive Holy Communion worthily if they so decide, having discussed the matter with a priest, and if they are convinced that their earlier marriage was invalid but not declared as such by the Church. The new Catechism says just the opposite. Yet the initial reaction from Rome was merely that there are "some problems" with these views.

On October 14, 1994, Cardinal Ratzinger, on behalf of the Congregation for the Doctrine of the Faith, formally rejected the view of these three German bishops, who immediately accepted the doctrinal position of the Holy See. It is clear from their response, however, that they intend to continue seeking some flexibility in this matter, lending comfort thereby to those theologians, here and abroad, who look upon their action, taken in 1993 without prior consultation with Rome, as a bellwether for future compromise in Church teaching or practice. In the meantime parish priests and laity, in the first world at least, will continue to be buffetted by contradictory pastoral counsel within Catholic circles, not only about the reception of Holy Communion by invalidly married Catholics, but also about the indissolubility of marriage itself. (See *Origins,* October 27, 1994.) That pattern of confusion is already evident in Germany, where press reports indicate that displeasure with Rome's interference in the local church's pastoral decision extends to high-ranking Catholic political figures.

Over the centuries Rome has developed a style of dealing with errant bishops, one that typically contains a large amount of good sense—at least before the arrival of the electronic media. While suspension and excommunication have occurred at times, traditional Vatican diplomacy with bishops involves "finesse", an adroit move quietly made to contain damage to souls, a private but stern dressing-down by the Pope or his delegate, the appointment of an auxiliary or co-adjutor to rein in excesses or to bring new enthusiasm to a worn-out administration, an extended trip for the prelate to Rome or around the world or to a clinic, and occasionally early retirement. Many of these "old tricks" were used, sparingly at least, from the early days of the Church's post–Vatican II systemic breakdown. But miscalculations and faulty decisions also occurred, based on the assumption that newer bishops, like the old, would bow to the wishes of the Pope.

Probably the outstanding *cause célèbre* of rebellion was the "Hunthausen Affair". Rome had been advised years before not to make him the archbishop of Seattle, following his dubious administration of the diocese of Helena. But Rome paid no heed to the advice. (More than one Catholic thinks that ecclesial promotion has sometimes gone—through cronyism—to someone whose doctrinal convictions were less than fully Catholic.) The archbishop of Seattle, for one, made a fetish of being "mod" in personal style, in liturgical practice, and in teaching. He was his own rule. Early in the game, he removed a pastor for objecting to diocesan catechetical material and, upon the priest's successful appeal to Rome, was ordered to restore the man to the pastoral office. That priest never again ran a parish. Hunthausen fed into all the causes that disturbed Paul VI and froze out of influence all those who could be called Catholic loyalists. Rome bumbled through a badly divided archdiocese until Hunthausen finally retired. But the appeasement process, involving the Church's cardinals, taught the wrong lesson to the entire American Church.

The appointment of adequate and competent bishops is no easy task in a universal Church. In prosperous and peaceful times, inadequacy and incompetence do not threaten the institutional well-being, if they are distributed carefully. But in times of turmoil, these shortcomings breed disaster, especially if bishops succumb to temptations to please antiauthority activists. Immediately after the Council, two young bishops quit their posts and told the world why. They were in love. While the Vatican's screening process tends to favor "quiet men"—those who give no sign of being potential troublemakers—classy or irenic appearances do not necessarily good bishops make. Some priests reach the episcopacy without anyone really knowing what their convictions are. Some are not theologically sophisticated although charming as movie stars. Years ago, the Pope bestowed an American archdiocese on a priest over the objections of his major advisors in Rome. The man had had no significant pastoral experience in the United States up to that moment. He has caused more than a few difficulties since.

Pio Laghi once announced the appointment of a bishop, only to learn that the priest had earlier publicly questioned the Church's teaching on the ordination of women. Embarrassed when asked for an explanation, the Pro-Nuncio replied: "I talked to him." To which his guest said: "You have only touched the tip of his particular iceberg." Raw power exercised by highly placed prelates, like Cardinal Dearden, introduced strange priests to the role of "successor to the apostles", over the objections of the Pope's chief advisors. During days of ecclesial malaise, the most troublesome bishops may be those who talk with the clear voice of a Catholic Jacob but whose hands of Esau give away what they verbally commit themselves not to do.

Timidity in governing, if untreated, becomes a contagious disease. Cardinal Terence Cooke, a gentle soul and potentially a firmer shepherd than he became, regularly faced intransigent opposition from priests and religious with the comment: "If Paul VI doesn't deal with this kind of conduct at higher levels, what can I do?"

Very little is said these days in favor of strong bishops who are in perfect union with the Pope, the kind that made the American Church what she became. When anything is said on that subject at all, it is said disparagingly.

Few cardinals endured the pain of heroic witness more than Patrick A. O'Boyle, who made it clear in 1968 that *Humanae vitae* was an important teaching instrument for the archdiocese of Washington. Priests there, numbering from nineteen to fifty, depending on when the count was made, made it obvious to their bishop that they would not serve on this basis. The Archbishop properly replied "No" to this challenge, thereby joining the issue at its root, viz., the fidelity of a priest with diocesan faculties to the teaching of the Church. Months earlier O'Boyle had made a telling point about the proportionalist mentality among the clergy. "If priests think that way, many will act that way." The Washington Cardinal was not a martinet, however. He spent uncountable hours interviewing each of those priests, some of whom left the priesthood. But he stuck to the Church's guns. He was the Church's custodian.

At the November 1968 bishops' meeting, O'Boyle was asked to report his experience to the assembly, at the conclusion of which an archbishop friend stood up to recommend that the episcopal body go on record in support. O'Boyle rose to his feet immediately, excusing his brother bishops from worrying about a problem that was his alone. As he later remarked: "It wasn't that I couldn't use support. But I wasn't too sure what I would get, and it would have been a greater scandal if only half the bishops had supported me." (Cardinal Dearden was not in his corner, and neither was the NCCB treasurer, Co-Adjutor Archbishop John J. Maguire, who normally tolerated little nonsense within the New York jurisdiction.)

However, O'Boyle's problems did not end there. Abetted by the Curran apparatus at CUA, the offending priests appealed to Rome, and three years later (April 26, 1971) Cardinal Wright sent back Rome's final word on the subject, defending O'Boyle's reasoning and conduct, but recommending an amicable return of the offending priests to duty. The Washington Archbishop was not amused that the offenders were required to make neither a confession of fault nor an act of contrition. O'Boyle blamed Wright for the oversight. Later, Vincent Mallon, M.M., explained that Paul VI specifically directed Wright *not* to impose any penalties.

Down through the years, Paul's successor has visited the United States on many occasions. While no one has to agree with that body of opinion which says that John Paul II has been variously insulted by the kinds of people officially designated to speak to him on behalf of the Catholic faithful in the United States, the appearance and conduct of these people, particularly at the Los Angeles meeting of 1987, certainly have been strange. The bishops in charge of those proceedings would be the first to take great umbrage if, on an official visit within their own dioceses, some pastor subjected one of them to presentations which indicated that their ordinary was leading the diocese astray. John Paul II was well equipped rhetorically on those occasions to do battle with his carefully selected critics, like the priest who was asking him to look more favorably on married clergy and women priests. With a smile on his face, the Pope cited the words of a popular World War I song: "It's a long way to Tipperary."

The institutional response of the Pope and his Roman Curia to the problems being created by national chanceries, not mere dialogue alone, will stimulate the recovery of Church well-being. It is not clear as of this moment, however, that the Pope is certain how to bring his many battles for the *magisterium* to a victorious conclusion. He still has internal difficulties. To cite one example: recently the president of the Fellowship of Catholic Scholars wrote to Cardinal Pio Laghi, prefect of the Congregation for

Catholic Education, suggesting that the "ordinances" for Catholic colleges and universities prepared by the American bishops and working their way through consultative processes of our National Conference were meaningless. Laghi replied by telling Ralph McInerny to take his concerns to those college presidents who were the bishops' chief advisors. This prompted the Fellowship's President Emeritus to tell Laghi that his letter to McInerny was bad advice and counterproductive to the best interests of the Church. It typified the counsel given early on to a politician about the country's Watergate problem: "Take it up with Haldeman or Erlichmann!" This was not the advice given twenty years ago by Cardinal Garrone, fighting Land O' Lakes college presidents, who today have, as they then had, the support of the ruling bishops of the National Conference.

Quite naturally, bishops need never be overfriendly with their critics. And those associated with policies that seem to have ener-vated Church piety are understandably hostile to those who threaten to obstruct their programs. Yet, a critic may be a true friend, while a constructive cooperator in little-understood change may be an enemy of the very bishops who expect loyalty. Even so, criticism of the NCCB has been at times severe, beginning with that given by the Pope, and harsh at the level of those Catholics who are antiestablishment by nature or by choice. For some of this, the responsible officials have only themselves to blame. They designed the Church of Vatican II aborning, and they harvested experts on their side who were champions of the changes they had in mind. From 1966 onward, most experts who read the Council documents differently were effectively quaran-tined as outsiders to the planned reforms. And the outsiders included bishops who might prove to be antivoices to the controlling leadership. During those early postconciliar days, the Roman Curia was also kept at bay. The new Church was collegial only in one direction.

The controversies that ensued were not mere rhetorical debates, and this explains why they were so heated. The truth on which the whole Catholic case rests depends exclusively on the living witness of Christ and that of the Church's *magisterium*. Philip Hughes once remarked that "the history of the Church confirms the teaching of the Church." This may be true if he had in mind the constant witness of bishops in union with the Pope; but it would not be true in regions where the ideas of Arius, William of Occam, John Calvin, or Alfred Loisy held sway among bishops and people. For at least a century, the vibrant American Church was relatively free from the baneful effects of the proposed "reforms" that did little to reinvigorate the Church of Europe, battered and worn as she was from the "isms" that divided that continent in the sixteenth century and after. Those same forces, unleashed anew during and after Vatican II, required careful handling, but the governance of the Church turned out to be anything but careful.

Part of our difficulties developed out of the Council's own ambiguities, those considered trifling or unsubstantial at the time, but which nonetheless became conduits through which ideas and policies which blurred Catholic identity were transmitted and which weakened the ability of the hierarchy to manage its own *aggiorniamento*. Henri de Lubac even thought that the simple reduction of episcopal consecration to an "ordination" was an attempt to situate bishops on a lower plane. Dropping the terms "primary" and "secondary" in describing the different ends of marriage was defended as a way of saying that there was more to matrimony than raising a family. But, once done, it did not take long for the theological establishment and matrimonial tribunals to make "marital love", for all practical purposes, the primary objective, thereby opening a way to tolerate, if not to justify, contraceptive practices, easy annulments (in some cases more than one for a given person), and out-of-the-closet homosexuality. "Religious freedom" against state coercion in matters religious became "academic freedom", liberating Catholic theologians and college presidents from episcopal supervision, even though the science of Catholic theology depends, not on theological argument, but on its "obedience of faith".

Bishops-in-the-field, in those early years, hardly knew what was going on within their own machinery. Those who made efforts to intervene in the internal affairs of the NCCB found out (to use Thomas Reese's phrase) that they were expected to be "team players". When the president of the Conference sent on to them *gratis* a copy of Reese's book *Archbishop,* a favorable commentary subtitled "Inside the Power Structure of the American Catholic Church", it never occurred to most of them why they were not similarly favored with the writings of Germain Grisez, Thomas Dubay, or William May. When the NCCB's catechetical journal *Living Light* was removed from the publication lists of *Our Sunday Visitor,* few bishops were aware that OSV's publisher was unhappy with the Catholicity of its content. When bad hospital guidelines were recalled and professions of faith never saw the light of day, few bishops were directly involved. And the priorities chosen by the Conference itself, the innovations that did not work or did harm (e.g., general absolution, First Communion before Penance), were not decisions of bishops-in-the-field. To this day, the managers of the episcopal bureaucracy do not apologize for errors or failures. They are likely to blame the malaise and disunity, as one NCCB paper did, on Ralph McInerny, James Schall, and James Hitchcock.

The hassle over the universal catechism and liturgical translations are currently widening the range of hitherto narrowly defined "episcopal collegiality". Still, there are bishops who know that all is not yet well, who are on the fringes of their own bureaucracy, who appreciate Roman anxieties, who tend to put a good face on their Conference, who see many good things going on, and assure complainers that things are getting better. Other bishops, however, in confidential situations, deny that this is so and place some responsibility for the imbedded dissent on Rome's double signals.

This latter point introduces the outrage vented against Church authority by leaders of the group called "cultural Catholics". These are they who are baptized, who intend to ask for the last anointing at the end, who take some satisfaction in calling themselves Catholic, but boastfully claim they will pick and choose what to believe in or do between those extremities. And they are angry because only minor bishops, not the Pope, have given them a blessing. Andrew Greeley is an articulate spokesman for their understanding of Catholicity. John Paul II was hardly eighteen months in Peter's Chair when Greeley, in one of his syndicated columns (April 20, 1980), made this judgment:

> The authority structure of the Catholic Church is in a state of collapse. Almost every day I encounter priests, nuns and laypeople who refuse to take the official Church seriously as a teacher on any matter, large or small.

This sociologist, who only ten years earlier had been chosen by the NCCB to tell bishops all they needed to know about the state of the American priesthood, opined there that matters are worse under John Paul II than they were under Paul VI. Piety and devotion, in the Greeley view, are not necessarily correlated with "assent" and "obedience" to the teaching of the Church. (Or to Christ?) And he offers statistics to show that, as far as Catholics are concerned, he is right, while the Pope and the bishops who follow him are wrong. His own "cultural Catholicism" is, of course, quite prevalent among the Church's opinion-molders.

How did the American Church, considering her strength in 1960, fall into her present condition?

I once asked another consultant of the NCCB, during his earlier and better days, how he explained the fall of the Jesuits. And he answered quickly: "They were done in by their arrogance." Perhaps, too, we should look upon the present suffering of the Church as penance for our sins, even for our pride in earlier accomplishments. That the Church presently is in the dock—as

Christ was, as Paul was, as martyrs always are—should surprise few, even if the jailers are our very own. We deal here in the mystery of Christianity itself, always certain by faith, hope, and charity that Good Friday inevitably leads to Easter Sunday. So the faithful bear their crosses, a little-appreciated experience in a hedonist culture, and pray as if their future, and that of the Church, depended on Providence alone.

Still, as St. Francis would say again, our own work is cut out for us, since Christ intended his disciples to gain other disciples and to keep them faithful both in faith and obedience. The Church must abide cultural Catholics, as long as she does not give them the impression that they are good Catholics. We must also encourage patience among the faithful without having them begin to think that the truths and way of life proper to the Church are beyond defense or made to appear indefensible.

Humano modo, many theories are being offered about how the Church got into the present predicament, perhaps the most serious in her lifetime, now that electronic media, hardly friends of Christ, tend to proliferate bad news rather than good. Different Catholics obviously adhere to different theories.

The *"incompetence theory"* explains the Catholic crisis on the basis of faulty governance by the Church's leadership. A competent Church knows why she exists and what she is supposed to do, and she chooses appropriate leaders suitable for the responsibilities imposed upon them, leaders who know how to defend the Church from her internal and external enemies. Contemporary pessimists favor this explanation of the Catholic downfall.

An offshoot of that belief is the *"conspiracy theory"*, which alleges that an underground Church, bent on modernizing Catholic doctrine and policies, surfaced after Vatican II, formed alliances with segments of the hierarchy, who dominated the decisions that debilitated those ecclesial structures already in place without adding substantially to the piety and devotion of the baptized masses. This theory does not assume that somewhere lurking in dark corners was a Msgr. Marx or a Fr. Engels, those who created "cells" to engineer an ecclesial take-over. Rather, as Peter Berger might say it, "birds of a feather flocked together" ("breathed together") to pursue a common cause, one whose eventual power and appeal, at the time of the Council's convocation, were underestimated by higher Church authority. At least the hierarchy of that day proved incapable of channeling dissent and disobedience to helpful Catholic purposes. What resulted, in Peter Hebblethwaite's words, was a "runaway Church". Henri de Lubac, years before, was probably more right than wrong when he observed, "The Church has always drawn down upon herself the contempt of the elite." Certainly, "cultural Catholicism" would be the most modern manifestation of what was earlier commonplace in many so-called Catholic royal houses.

Enough evidence exists to satisfy those so inclined about the empirical basis for either of these theories. These theories may not explain fully the failure of those responsible for making John XXIII's vision come true. Yet they have currency. But recovery is not likely thirty years later, even if a détente could be arranged between the Church's *modernizers* and her *ecclesiasts*. In this case the truth of God's very Word would remain uncertain and the "assent" and "obedience" owed by Christians to that Word would become weasel words.

There is a third, and far more sinister, interpretation of Catholic malaise in what, for want of a better phrase, is called *"the hidden-agenda theory"*. This is a variation of the *"conspiracy theory"*, sinister because it goes beyond assumed capitulation by authority figures to superior force. It suggests, instead, that Catholic prelates are active collaborators in the revolutionary process. It alleges, further, that Rome is preparing to coopt "the Protestant principle", but in such a way as to avoid losing Catholic loyalists for the duration of their lifetime. These theorists point out how the Holy See keeps declaring Catholic principles absolutely but leaves their institutionalization to national bodies of bishops, with little follow-up to see if this is faithfully done. The appointment of classic-type Roman bishops is duly noticed by the media but mingled with a larger number of moderate types unlikely to disturb the status quo. Strong pronouncements on contraception are made regularly—avoiding, however, terminology that speaks of "sin"—and on the indissolubility of Christian marriage, but without serious intervention in the massive annulment actions by American tribunals. A quasi-infallible pronouncement in Rome on the nonordination of women followed earlier concessions to feminist-sensitive bishops, like the one who remarked, "I guess it shows the Vatican is obeying us." And so forth.

This theory, far-fetched as it is, is pondered by some in official quarters, who contemplate a Church of England writ Roman. While it draws heavily on sociological studies of creeping secularization in most modern religious institutions, it also underestimates the mystery of the Church's perdurance in her own faith. Why is it that time and again, if only at the last moment, the blood of martyrs and the witness of saints enliven anew the Body of Christ, whose living head lives in Rome?

Whatever the theory and however Providence is playing out God's intervention in Church history, this is the *realpolitik* facing John Paul II at the end of his pontificate and at the beginning of the one he will hand on to his inevitable successor.[2]

---

[2] Interestingly, Eamon Duffy's *Stripping of the Altars: Traditional Religion in England 1400–1580* (Yale University Press) makes a similar point when it suggests that the Protestant Reformation in England was forced on Catholic people by the powers-that-be, not by the free choice of the faithful.

Chapter Six

John Paul II vs. the Catholic College System

The Church is going nowhere, except in retreat, if her leadership does not find a way to win the war thrust upon her in 1967. Indeed, conditions may be worse in 1994 than they were in 1979. And will continue to be so, as long as important pastors think they can mediate issues that are nonnegotiable, or if they think war can be won without bloodshed, even without some of their own. Whole countries gave up their Catholic identity when that kind of thinking prevailed.

In some respects, the "1967 War of Catholic Elites" is comparable to World War II in the Pacific, a battle over islands leading to someone's homeland. If "the Curran debacle" was our Pearl Harbor, and "Land O'Lakes" a loss similar to that of the Philippines, the flight of religious orders from obedience to hierarchy remains the "Battle of Midway". Religious orders stand between the Pope and the academic establishment, especially its theologians.

The present Catholic war also has features in common with the Civil War, because affiliated ecclesial states are now willing to form "a more perfect union" with the universal Church only on terms agreeable to the states. The theological/university/order triad, which has been an intrinsic component of the universal Church from the Middle Ages, now wishes to reestablish itself as quasisovereignties, with whom the pastors of the Church must renegotiate their continued membership in that Church. Sufficient are the Jefferson Davises willing to do precisely this in our time.

Framing the contemporary Catholic situation in such terms may sound somewhat extreme to the "business as usual" ecclesial types. But, then, Winston Churchill was also more than a nuisance to Neville Chamberlain, and Franklin Delano Roosevelt had many unkind things to say about critics of his Japan policy, at least until his young countrymen were buried in blood. But our Pearl Harbor (Charles Curran) is now almost thirty years older, our Philippines (Land O'Lakes colleges) are still in the hands of insurgents, and our Midway (religious orders) can be recaptured only when we retake those institutional islands where obedient religious superiors once worked mainly for the successors of Peter and the apostles.

The present war, like all wars, is about turf. Who has the last word on any land spot that wishes to claim Catholic identity? Or on a campus where there may be a cross somewhere, but the institution serves purposes which a given pope may not recognize as authentically Catholic? The present war is the Protestant revolution writ differently. Back in the sixteenth century, private interpretation of God's Word by individuals became in theory everyone's religious right; in the twentieth century, it is private interpretation of God's Word by the Church's own substructures, which claim the right to proclaim God's Word independently and to become thereby legitimate rivals to the Church's universal pastors for followers. Such structural divisions beget a seemingly official high, low, and middle Catholicity, the type of doctrinal disunity which has reduced Protestantism to ineffectuality, but which is fundamentally inimical to a Christ who made it clear that those who opposed his apostles were also against him. Why should committed Catholic subinstitutional leaders find it easier today than the elders of old to render to God what belongs to God? Why should they not reject any demands of Caesar which impinge on their faith and choose instead to be a living witnesses (i.e., martyrs) to their professed faith?

Rehashing the travails of Paul VI and John Paul II since Vatican

II only serves one purpose: to help Catholics face the reality of a war now thrice as long as the Vietnam tragedy which befell our nation. If a "body count" in our war is never discussed, it is for the reason that no one has yet figured out how to make a "soul count". When Archbishop Oscar Lipscomb, former chairman of the NCCB's Doctrinal Committee, says, as he did recently, "When it comes to sound Catholic teaching in Catholic colleges, all is not well", he makes the understatement of the year.[1] As a notable religious once told a prelate who criticized his religious community for its uncanonical doings: "Bishop, you don't know the half of it."

But Lipscomb may have pointed a finger toward what might be our inevitable Normandy Beach. To protect the Church's future, our bishops will eventually have to land somewhere on Catholic college campuses, whose fortresses, embattlements, and self-defense mechanisms, aimed at the hierarchy, are already set in concrete. The recovery of general Catholic integrity and order demands a breakthrough on those shores.

Bishop James Malone also made reference to the rationale used by our colleges to remain autonomous.[2] God forbid that they "be seen as nothing more than an extension of the ministry of the bishop". But what else are they, if they be truly Catholic, but extensions of the ministry of the Church, spiritually as well as intellectually, and of whose Catholicity the bishop, if he is a good bishop, is the ultimate guardian? Did Catholic colleges come into being to serve government or to please accrediting agencies or to accumulate public wealth and influence?

On January 1, 1798, Georgetown College, the first institution of higher education in the United States, stated in its prospectus its principal objectives:

> Persuaded that irreligion and immorality in a youth, portend the most fatal evils to subsequent periods of life, and threaten

[1] *Origins,* February 17, 1994, p. 609.
[2] Ibid., p. 608.

even to disturb the peace, and corrupt the manners of society at large; the directors of this Institution openly profess that they have nothing so much at heart as to implant virtue, and destroy in their pupils the seeds of vice—Happy in the attainment of this sublime object, they would consider the success in this alone, as an ample reward for their incessant endeavors.

The word "college" is not an abstraction. It is the highest unit in someone's system of education—state, secularist, Protestant, Catholic, even communist. Whose ownership sets the tone? Which ideology defines "academic freedom" and "institutional autonomy"? What philosophy controls the disbursement of government money? Why should a fully believing Catholic president, true to the mission of his founders, give up his institution's birthright for the pottage offered by unbelievers of one kind or another?

Once upon a time a Catholic alumnus, after identifying himself, might add embarrassingly: "I'm not very good at it, though." Today, his son or daughter might qualify their identity differently and with a certain hauteur: "Of course, I don't agree with everything the Church teaches." Once many of the very best practicing Catholics in the United States were the graduates of Catholic colleges; today, graduates who retain their faith are still plentiful, but the ones who trouble pastors most are the majority who think and act as if the Church were irrelevant to their worldly life. In former days, the faith was at the center of a Catholic school's life, even in the mathematics class. At lunch time the students argued its meaning, perhaps after hearing a dull professor's bad arguments in its defense. Students then, however, heard the same religious thing everywhere, even Christ's "hard sayings". Today, students want "freedom" and "autonomy" above the Church's truth because their professors think of these as the chief attributes of an enlightened Catholic. Archbishop Fulton Sheen's dictum a generation ago still has relevancy: "I tell my relatives to send their teenagers to secular colleges where they will have to fight for their faith rather than to Catholic colleges where it will be stolen from them."

Within the scope of federal law or the rules of accrediting agencies, ample room exists to be fully Catholic and to demand the full benefits that belong to American citizens, especially the right to choose (or establish) a fully committed Catholic college. If college presidents or boards appear to favor only a nominal or tepid Catholicity, the ever-growing omni-competent government, and its subservient private satellites, will deny the Church and her members their constitutional rights. The stouthearted—today mostly small places like Thomas Aquinas in California and Ohio's Steubenville University—can turn out upwardly mobile, yet intensely believing and pious Catholics and scores of priests and religious that not even the bishop-owned Catholic University of America seems to foster.

A Normandy Beach of some kind is on the horizon for the American hierarchy if only because Pope John Paul II in 1990 issued a new law (apostolic constitution) for Catholic higher education. *Ex corde Ecclesiae* requires implementation by local hierarchies, through a system of "ordinances" or statutes which, by definition, would bind institutions who wish to claim a Catholic identity. The Pope hopes to restore the Catholic faith to the center of any campus that trades on the Church's name. *Ex corde Ecclesiae* itself is the end result of a dialogic process that began worldwide in 1968. It requires, among other things, that the name Catholic be reserved to those schools so recognized by Church authority, that professors in the field of ecclesiastical science be licensed ("mandated"), somewhat after the fashion of doctors, engineers, and lawyers in civilized countries. Bishops are to keep an ongoing eye on the quality of the Catholic performance. (No such legislation was necessary in the 1917 Code of Canon Law, because religious superiors and college presidents, laymen included, could be trusted "to keep the faith", their own, their faculty's, their students, and the respect, too, of those non-Catholics who preferred to teach under Catholic auspices.) The first draft of "ordinances" to originate from the NCCB (1993) is meaningless, largely because it contains invitations, not demands. It is also deficient because it lacks the enforcement machinery customary for "ordinances" of any kind.

Rome's demands, repeatedly made on educators and bishops since 1972, receive less than full reception in the proposed ordinances. The following are basic to recovery:

1. No institution can claim the name *Catholic* without ecclesiastical approval.

2. The *Catholic* college must specify, in statutes and in contracts with personnel, its Catholicity and its adherence to norms of the faith determined by the *magisterium.*

3. The school must establish in its statutes a specific machinery for protecting the truths of the faith and the faith of the college community.

4. The teachers of ecclesiastical subjects must receive a "mandate" from competent ecclesiastical authority.

5. The institution's autonomy is "interior", not exterior. The president or board manages the college, but, since the school is in and of the Church, the bishop or bishops may make observations or remonstrations, if need be, to a professor, to the president, or to the Catholic public, whenever the situation so requires.

Most of these demands have up to now come from Rome in the form of requests, seeking voluntary adoption at local levels. They have been benignly neglected over the years. One commonly hears bishops say, "I can't mandate that", or "I can't do this." But they say this mostly when they are likely to have a fight on their hands from insurgents. They do mandate regularly, whenever the subjects of their ordinances are docile. Bishops also mandate when they permit ongoing evil situations to develop or to become institutionalized as prescriptive rights against Church supervision. More than one educator believes that the secularization of Catholic higher education has too far gone to be reversed on most campuses. On the other hand, both Charles Curran and Hans Küng, and Anthony Kosnik's *Human Sexuality,* for all practical purposes, have been marginalized within the Church by ecclesial decree. These names may still receive passing notice, but they can no longer claim ecclesiastical approval, as they once did, because they had Catholic employment. We can thank Rome for the remedial censures, even though they arrived many years after the real damage to the Church occurred.

The very thought of impending "ordinances" means that the effective re-entry of Catholic bishops onto Catholic campuses is more than a pious wish. Will the bishops be emboldened to enter that privileged Church sanctuary forthrightly from which they have been excluded for so long to the detriment of souls? Or, will *Ex corde Ecclesiae* become as irrelevant on college campuses as *Humane vitae* is in certain theology departments? Richard McCormick has already relegated *Veritatis splendor* to the ecclesial heap in which, he claims, Pius XII's *Humani generis* has been buried for four decades.

The spade-work done so far by the NCCB to have their "ordinances" move effortlessly onto Catholic campuses is not very promising, if early proposals are any indication.

Bishop John Leibrecht, who chairs the NCCB's ad hoc committee for implementing *Ex corde Ecclesiae,* made the following statements to the annual meeting of the Association of Catholic Colleges and Universities (February 2, 1994):

1. The Church is "significantly enriched by Catholic colleges and universities".

2. *Ex corde Ecclesiae* is "generally welcomed by Catholic colleges and universities in the United States".

3. The basic relationship of bishops and Catholic colleges "should remain informal and dialogic in nature".

4. *Ex corde Ecclesiae* states the bishop is not related to the college's "internal governance".

5. The bishop's relationship to a college is one "of communion, not of control".

6. Ordinances need not be seen in a negative light.

7. Ordinances must respect academic freedom and institutional autonomy.

8. The bishop's role is unique in protecting Catholic teaching and practice.

9. Some bishops wonder if informal procedures of supervision are effective.

10. It is difficult to implement a mandate for theology professors.

11. Ordinances should be few.

12. Ordinances should be acceptable not only to bishops and the Holy See but to the ACCU as well.

13. We must search for relationships; that is the question.

A number of these statements are incontrovertible, but many others are dangerous evasions constructed to appease ACCU officials. At least two do not accord with reality. College presidents object strenuously to the proposed ordinances, even though in present form they are hardly stern demands. They do not like the symbolism of bishops looking over their shoulders, even in matters of faith and worship. Furthermore, autonomy from episcopal oversight makes their continuing enrichment of the Church dubious. Catholic worship and its offspring, piety, necessary by-products of faith, require communion with the bishop and, in a certain sense, develop under his supervision. Whether Catholic presidents like it or not, this gives him a certain external control, which requires them to behave in a certain way, if they choose to be Catholic.

Civil lawmakers do not run universities. And, prior to enacting statutes of any kind, they consult interested parties. Yet, what democratic Congress, intent on protecting public health, or human rights, or national security, or the state's interests in the proper education of its citizens, would so frame legislation that doctors, CEOs, generals, or university presidents, after enactment, were free to determine when, how, or if the law applied to them? Statutes are sometimes difficult to draft, to fashion into regulations, to enforce. But, however it works out, law tilts everyone's public behavior toward the common, not the private, good. Lawmaking designed to correct evil embedded in society overcomes these difficulties or it is meaningless. Nowhere does Bishop Leibrecht mention the evils episcopal ordinances are supposed to remedy.

Another aspect of an approach that will not work is that, for all the talk of "open Church" and "dialogue", our bureaucracies usually converse sympathetically—and *Origins* duly reports the results—with critics and enemies of the *magisterium*. Rarely are recognized Catholic apologists invited to "dialogue". The alliance of bureaucrats and dissidents goes back to Charles Curran's days. While Curran was under censure, he asked a perfectly legitimate question: Why pick on me? Catholic theology departments everywhere were already filled with his likes. Small groups of bishops have held meetings with college presidents other than those in control of the Association of Catholic Colleges and Universities. Yet they have often appeared helpless to do more than nod at complaints against the status quo and unable to change the course charted by the Dearden-Bernardin entente. Now, a quarter-century after Rome began to insist on bishops exercising their responsibility over Catholic colleges, a first step is about to be taken.

When similar issues emerged during the Council, and thereafter, a lonely Vincentian priest, now the retired president of St. John's University (1965–1989), rose to confront the original Hesburgh-Henle combine, on behalf of the Holy See. Here is how Joseph T. Cahill, C.M., stated the case thirty years ago (1965). His arguments are just as valid now, even if they are couched in his own university's perspective:

> St. John's University regards it as a solemn duty at this time to reaffirm its position as a Roman Catholic institution of higher learning. . . . This trust means that St. John's University must adhere not only to the highest standards of excellence, but also to the teaching, legislation, and spirit of the Roman Catholic Church. Nothing whatsoever shall be allowed to compromise this resolve (SJU Archives, October 25, 1965).

As of 1976, when the secularization of Catholic higher education looked like it was all but complete, Cahill reviewed the results of "Land O' Lakes":

> While many alumni of Catholic institutions are "loyal and grateful to their colleges," there are also large numbers of alumni presently unhappy with what is happening to their sons and daughters on Catholic campuses, unhappiness which is shared by pastors of souls, up to and including Pope Paul VI. Whether future alumni will be "loyal and grateful" is a matter of some concern.
>
> Too much stress is placed on government aid for the survival of authentic Catholic education of quality. Granted, if the price is right, government support is always desirable. . . . While [NCEA's] draft statement acknowledges the rights of secular society over higher education, it does not support sufficiently the rights of the Church and hierarchy, who represent the common good of the Church.
>
> Alternatives to reliance on government for survival are never easy. But there *are* alternatives, one of which is eschewing public funds which can be had only at the expense of formal Catholic identity and Catholic performance.
>
> Accrediting agencies in the United States judge an institution on what of itself it professes to be according to its own

statutes. They take the Catholic profession into account. Furthermore, professional unionization of faculty, as at St. John's University, also recognizes the Catholic commitment which accompanies hiring. . . .

It is no longer true in the American world [that] educational "control" is exercised basically by the educators themselves. Government, foundation, and professional bureaucracies have a large and increasing role. There is no reason, therefore, why only Church authority's role should be minimal (SJU Archives, February 23, 1976).

A year earlier (1975), the president of the NCCB was asked by Fr. Cahill to face the harsh reality he was already experiencing even before Vatican II had completed its work:

At the heart of the dispute (1965) was an attempt to eliminate all substantive relationships between the University and the Catholic Church, and to deny the authority of the Board of Trustees to identify any areas wherein the status of the University as a religious institution might influence teaching. St. John's fought off this attack alone, and that of the academic world, Catholic and secular, with very few exceptions, and with minimal help from Church authorities (SJU Archives, November 14, 1975).

Gabriel Cardinal Garrone, Rome's prefect for Catholic Education, approved Fr. Cahill's conduct:

The statement that you made to Archbishop Bernardin and the NCCB Administrative Committee is a remarkable document for its candid and respectful presentation of facts and its sincere recourse to bishops. We are deeply delighted by both these aspects (SJU Archives, November 29, 1975).

In the end, both Cardinal Garrone and Fr. Cahill were ignored by the NCCB Committee.

The Catholic campus in 1994 remains the point where all the Church's advanced specialties intersect, from which for good or for ill, the Church will draw her future leadership. In bygone years converts enriched the Church, those whose background was once totally Protestant or secular. By and large, however, the hard-won glory of American Catholicity, carping critics to the contrary notwithstanding, was due mainly to the quality, infused faith, and discipline of its own educators, to whom assent and obedience were more noble virtues than the secular respectability or independence of bishops. If, in the future, priests, religious, theologians, canonists, editors, catechists, dramatists, and lay leaders depend for their lifelong mind-set on secularist opinion-molders, especially if these are acquired in schools still graced by the cross but hardly cross-bearing, then the prospects of a pious Church, a holy Church, and a general state of grace at the parish level are not particularly bright. And, when we say this, we mean that the Church's creeds will no longer be controlling Catholic lives.

Certain conclusions may be fairly drawn from the previous review:

1. The battle for the American Church has been going on too long. Its ill-effect on the religious life of the faithful, especially of the young, and on the unity of the Church is deleterious, even if offending circles pretend otherwise.

2. The source of the Church's difficulties was, and continues to be, campuses which call themselves Catholic but which, by their own confession, no longer choose to teach or defend Catholic faith and morals as these are authentically taught by Pope and bishops or to obey sections of Canon Law applying to them.

3. We forget that strong university presidents, who controlled their boards, separated their institutions from the overview of bishops. In spite of animadversions to the contrary, strong Catholic presidents can restore in their boards and faculties a respect for obedience to their Catholic patrimony.

4. The Holy See, for a quarter of a century, has tried valiantly, but unsuccessfully, to persuade Catholic college presidents voluntarily to adopt norms and measures of self-definition

and self-regulation which would guarantee the integrity of the faith and the Catholic life-style of those who work or study in their institutions.

5. More than ten years ago the Holy See began to establish policies, culminating in *Ex corde Ecclesiae* (1990), that call for ecclesial recognition of colleges which wish to call themselves Catholic, licensing (mandates) for professors of ecclesiastical studies, and continued oversight by the hierarchy of performance which may affect adversely the well-being of the faithful.

6. Every society, the Church not excluded, is responsible for the well-being of its constituent membership, when necessary through charters, leases, licenses, and periodic government oversight. Since, therefore, Catholic colleges are so vital to the evangelization procedures of the Church, there is no reason why the Church authority may not demand conformity to Church law to a degree no less binding than that presently exacted from these institutions by federal and state governments.

7. Bishops in executive session, following counsel from a committee of bishops with experience in Catholic higher education and from congregations in Rome, including Doctrine of the Faith, should establish necessary and true ordinances to be promulgated at an appropriate time.

(By the end of 1993, leading members of the Association of Catholic Colleges and Universities made it clear that the weak "ordinances" proposed to them earlier that year by an NCCB committee were unacceptable, and they so informed their faculties. As a consequence, the Committee chairman, Bishop Leibrecht, went back to the drawing board, deciding that "ordinances", strictly required by *Ex corde Ecclesiae,* were perhaps inopportune, inappropriate, and not likely to gain compliance from the American system of Catholic higher education. So on July 8, 1994, the Chairman called for another round of dialogue by bishops and academics on the nature and function of the Catholic identity, the Catholic college, and the Catholic episcopacy, all questions which have been studied, here and in Rome, interminably. *Ex corde Ecclesiae* [now four years old] had hoped to resolve these questions in favor of the Church's teaching and governing authority.

The reason modern society is so badly divided, and frequently lawless, is because government officials have developed the habit of allowing special interests to prevail over the common good. A community eternally restudying "questions", in the face of evident and immediate public evil, is badly served by its government. If, after a quarter of a century of studying crime with a view to legislation, a presidential commission recommends that more time be given to defining crime, or the role of the federal or state government, or whether special interests should have veto power over the final meaning or implementation of public law, it would be clear that government no longer governs. Asking at this date what the Catholic identity is, what a Catholic college is, what a bishop's role in the Church is, is magisterial futility, to say the least.)

8. College and university presidents should be given a fixed time to indicate their acceptance of these norms and a reasonable period to adjust their catalogues and operating procedures accordingly.

9. Institutions that do not choose to accept these ordinances are to be denied use of the name *Catholic.* The faithful are entitled to know the names of those institutions accredited by bishops as Catholic. The Church may lose a goodly number of colleges in the process. Let them go.

Just as the state sets standards for the charters under which an institution may function as a college or university, so may the

Church, if only as a measure of defense in perilous times, determine minimum standards for institutions bearing the name Catholic. If Catholic hospitals may not perform abortions, and Catholic youth hostels may not permit homosexual behavior, there is no reason why a Catholic college may hire or maintain on staff professors who lead the young into sins against faith and morals or into religious indifference. Administrations must defend their selectivity before the world on the basis of their right to be more than nominally Catholic.

If state departments of education can examine the credentials of faculty, the quality of libraries, the way government money is spent, and place limits on experimentations with biological or environmental consequences, even those conducted without public monies, why is an analogous oversight denied the highest authorities of the Church when the experimenters in religious matters are a threat to the faith of Catholics?

Federal law gives ample room for freedom of religion if institutions pursue it zealously. In some cases, the truly Catholic college must foreswear compromising entanglements with government. And if secular accrediting agencies step beyond proper bounds, Church officers, like the rabbinate earlier, may set up their own accreditation system under federal law.

The difficulties at this time of enacting or enforcing ordinances are the Church's own fault. "Laissez-faire" is one ideology that ill-befits Church authority in the exercise of its religious responsibility. Yet, for more than a generation this is precisely the philosophy under which American bishops have permitted college presidents to function. Corporate presidents of all kinds consistently resist restrictions on their greed or on their criminal activity, the country's commonweal to the contrary notwithstanding. Today's Catholic college presidents are of this genre vis-à-vis the Pope and the bishops in union with him—in the latter's legitimate exercise of authority as vicars of Christ.

Almost thirty years after Land O' Lakes, discussions on given campuses about their Catholicity is either a charade or a sincere effort to reclaim a valuable patrimony long since wasted away. The theology department is bad, the school of religious studies is worse, the president shamelessly hires the most notorious dissenters or virulent feminists around, outspoken defenders of the *magisterium* are denied promotion or otherwise harassed or isolated, cohabitation may take place in dormitories, homosexual clubs may find a home, and so forth. In New York State, the pretense is legal. Any college which accepts "Bundy money" must declare itself nondenominational by law yet draw on its Catholic tradition to attract students and money to maintain the kind of campus ministry once reserved for colleges that represented no one's religious faith. What happens to the faith and morals of the constituency, to the reputation of the Church, and to the truth for whose search Land O' Lakes was first conceived, is relegated to the institutional subconscious. Catholicity survives as in a gulag.

But the Church, good mother that she is, has a knack of digging into the conscience even of her fallen-aways, and of corporations too, as long as the breath of Catholic life prevails among those who truly have faith and are willing to suffer for it. Sometimes what looked dead or dying has enough spark of life to encourage someone to try resuscitation, perhaps when a pope gives the word loudly enough, or after a Protestant scholar warns his Catholic colleagues what lies ahead for a dead religious university.

George Marsden, a believing Christian, left Duke University to accept a teaching assignment at Notre Dame University because he wanted to be part of a "school where religious questions were more central to the intellectual life of the institution". As the author of a masterpiece called *The Soul of the American University,* Marsden documents in horrible detail how Protestant universities lost their souls long ago. Not by any cosmic decision, he assures us, but by minor choices to be more like God-less universities than witnesses to Martin Luther or John Calvin. His word "soul" is well chosen, because without a soul a body has no worthwhile life. It is the *anima* of a university which defines its *persona moralis,* not merely for the purpose of discussing questions but to animate the entire *corpus.* Marsden thinks Catholic universities are where Protestant universities were in 1930—on the downward road to secularization. In the Catholic case, secularization has profound and ominous significance for the Catholic Church, which defines herself differently from the way various Protestant churches do.

How far the Catholic college has gone down that slippery road varies with the situation. *Notre Dame News* asks the question: "Can Notre Dame be a great University and not lose its soul?" Some of its in-house respondents are not too sure if Catholicity is confined to selected quarters or events. Others think that a pervasive institutional Catholicity or too many pious Catholics might be a step backward, discouraging those who otherwise might patronize South Bend. At least the question is being debated. But while the debate continues, it is the function of public society to establish and enforce laws for the protection of the common good. In this case, the public society is the Church. And the biblical maxim applies: *Qui potest capere, capiat.*

Several years ago, Ignatius Press issued Donna Steichen's book *Ungodly Rage.* The title refers to the devilish anger of feminists against the patriarchal Church. But the title also fits larger numbers of dissident academics in their animus against the hierarchical Church, whether it be a Richard McBrien of Notre Dame blasting John Paul II for naming Thomas Daily bishop of Brooklyn, or a Michael J. Buckley, S.J., of Berkeley, accusing the Holy See of "material sin" in censuring pro-abortion nuns, or a Richard McCormick belittling John Paul II's moral absolutes. And "ungodly rage" is vented by the little-known classroom teachers of our young more often than bishops choose to acknowledge. The sole concern of bishops, at this moment of history, must be the state of Catholic marriages, the holiness of family life, the sacredness of worship and rituals, and the meaning of priesthood and religious life, all of which have been adversely affected by what often originates somewhere in a college or university. External governance, to which every citizen or Church member is subject, is somewhat normal, indeed effortless, when good will exists on both sides of the line of authority. It becomes difficult when bad will, even meanness, is entrenched on one side or the other. Bishops would be well advised to read Neil G. McCluskey's *The Catholic University: A Modern Appraisal* so as to discover how much ill will existed in Land O' Lakes by 1967. Church authority never did anything right in dealing with scholars, it averred, and any effort to oversee or restrain the work of Catholic academicians (in the words of McCluskey himself) "is basically irrational or immoral". In the absence of good will, disorder and disrespect for constituted authority naturally proceed from teachers to students to the body ecclesiastic, for which bishops alone bear responsibility, for its continuance or for its eventual elimination.

More than that, intense faith in Jesus Christ and "his Word" is endangered. For some strange reason, Churchmen rarely speak any more—at least in concrete terms—of "loss of faith" or of "bad Catholics". Speaking of the "one, true Church" has also gone out of style because it sounds anti-ecumenical or "fundamentalist", the assumption being that it is gauche to assert any more that Christ did have a specific and separate Church in mind, one that was to be his unto eternity. Many years ago, leading American theologians were hard-pressed in *America* magazine to define the word "heresy", let alone specify where it might be found in the Vatican II Church. Denial of Christ's divinity might do it, but not necessarily, if it is merely a matter of reexplaining Nicaea or Chalcedon against those Councils' original meanings. Yet, certainly, "pick and choose" Catholicity, already institutionalized in vast areas of the Catholic community, neatly fits under the etymology of the Greek word *haeresis.* One would have to be a Rip Van Winkle not to know that, within a generation, vital Catholic teachings have been redefined at lower levels of the Church, contrary to the teachings represented by the new *Catechism of the Catholic Church.*

The Catholic faith has also been compromised by the frequent
appeal, even by bishops, to "pastoral practice" over against "dogmatic
or moral principle". As if deliberately disbelieving or directly
doing evil can ever be legitimized by casuistry or compassion. It is
one thing after the fact to "suffer with" the sinner, especially in the
confessional or the rectory office; quite another to mount a pulpit
or write a column or a letter which leaves parishioners feeling that
God so understands their personality and circumstances that, for
them, believing or doing wrong is believing or doing right. This
obfuscation, if seemingly permitted by the *magisterium,* raises
serious questions about whether the Church may subtly be
suggesting that, as teacher of God's Word, she might have been
wrong all along. If one Catholic learns this from a pastor, other
Catholics also become entitled to place their conscientious decision above the words of Christ himself, as if by prescriptive right
acquired over time. And so over time, religious doubt, at the least,
and moral evil are institutionalized in the Body of Christ instead
of faith and virtue.

This dichotomy between pastoral practice and Catholic truth,
once institutionalized in the Church politic, undermines the very
notion that Christ or his Church has anything to say which binds
the minds or conduct of those who say they believe in Christ and
the Church as true. The issue is far more serious than in 1987,
when a group of afficionados of the idea within the USCC
structure told the Pope face to face that they wanted to negotiate
what they, as Church members, need accept from him as Catholic
obligation. Their rationale at the time was that educated Americans have the right to make up their own minds on matters critical
to their lives. They were, of course, defending the "pick and
choose" Catholicity John Paul II had condemned as inconsistent
with the Catholic faith commitment.

But the very notion of "God's Word" or "God's Law", certainly of revelation, is eviscerated totally of significant meaning if
and when Church authority itself is reluctant to or fails to specify

certain conduct or proclivities as sinful or disordered. The "pastoral-practice-divorced-from-the-truth syndrome", as practiced today in many places, calls for compassion, even forgiveness, for people who do in fact represent a disordered way of life or an immoral behavior pattern. You work to reconcile a contraceptive user but never tell him that he is a sinner, or you tell a lesbian to be chaste but never that homosexuality is a disorder. The matter transcends the Sixth Commandment. A nonviolent member of organized crime or a laid-back member of a rabid theology department undercutting the faith of students may not engage in sinful acts personally, but their situation is disordered or, as we used to say, objectively evil.

When Christ told the woman taken in adultery, "Go, sin no more" (Jn 8:11), he did not leave her in ignorance of the sin of adultery, about which he had a great deal to say. St. Paul was quite clear about this matter in Romans 6:16–17:

> Do you not know that if you present yourselves to some-one as obedient slaves, you are the slaves of the one you obey, either of sin, which leads to death, or of obedience which leads to righteousness, but thanks be to God that, al-though you were once slaves of sin, you have become obedient from the heart to the pattern of teaching to which you were entrusted.

A Christian, especially a pastor or theologian, cannot avoid God's Word about sin or about the states and conditions which lead to sin. This important truth underlies the virtues of justice and mercy.

Bishop Norman McFarland of Orange, after a visit with the Pope, may report John Paul's message to California bishops, "Preach the truth." But, if it is possible in pastoral practice to fudge the truth or ignore its existence, then that message becomes vanity of vanities. Canon 528 insists that pastors "see to it that the Christian faithful are instructed in the truths of the faith". But this does not occur when, in the face of activist opposition so common in our time, silence reigns in Catholic pulpits or in Church quarters about moral evil or disorder.

Many years ago, Richard McCormick, S.J., spoke about "the *magnum silentium*" over birth control. But as a result of the same kind of activism that prevailed then, the impossibility of priestly ordination of women, the necessity of private Confession and a state of grace for the worthy reception of Communion, the indissolubility of marriage, among other Christian truths, are today open questions for many Catholics. Similarly, the pastoral care of the divorced, of homosexuals, and of criminals will continue to be flawed if those caught up in difficult human situations come to feel that the old Church was wrong, rigid, and inhuman, while the new Church is more responsive to the difficulties in their lives. Still, the Catholic Church, while serving people's legitimate needs, may not satisfy their wants any more than Christ did, especially if these wants are objectively evil or disordered. The "pastoral-practice-divorced-from-the-truth syndrome" allows Catholics to think that the Church, under pressure, will relax her claim to speak anymore of the truth about God's Word if it proves inconvenient to certain categories of people.

Christians ultimately choose their way of life—in conformity with or opposed to the Word of God. But they cannot create the truth contained in God's Word or change it. That teaching has a commanding force of its own, which even pastors may not ignore or veto. John Paul II's effort in the new Catechism and in *Veritatis splendor* is not worldly counsel but the Word of God. For decades in many European college settings, observers often wondered about one or the other professor: "He can't have any faith left." Many were convinced that some of their peers no longer accepted Jesus Christ as the Son of God, or the Church as his authoritative voice. The most notorious case of that kind involved Alfred Loisy, Modernist biblical scholar in the first decade of the twentieth century, who said Mass every day until he was excommunicated.

Only then did he confess that he had not believed in the Real Presence for years. Dealing with lack of faith in Catholic institutions is no less and even more a problem today for bishops than for college presidents. Committed Catholic presidents have a personal or parochial obligation to remedy that situation; the onus on bishops is official and divinely imposed, not only to contain such confusion within their institutions but to confront promptly the error with vigorous argumentation. Neither of these remedies has been commonplace in recent years.

Bishops of this era, therefore, have a harder time bishoping than their predecessors. Bishop Lawrence Casey admitted as much, leaving Rochester in 1966, as auxiliary, to become ordinary of Paterson, New Jersey. When congratulated by his mentor Bishop James Kearney (the first prelate to fire Charles Curran), Casey replied: "No. You've had joy in your thirty and more years as bishop. From here on it will only be pain, pure and simple." And so it is. Still, in the Catholic scheme of things, bishops, they and they above all, are responsible for its growth and decline. In good times hardly any Catholic knows how important bishops are; in bad times they bear the brunt of criticism. It cannot be otherwise. Some of the criticism will be in poor taste, other will be directed at the wrong bishops or at the right ones for the wrong reason. Shrill and mean-spirited voices make everyone uncomfortable, especially if the critics are defending the wrong causes. The more objectionable critics, and the most dangerous, are those who hold bishops hostage to terror by threats of violence against the Church.

Fear of rupture, of public infamy, perhaps of schism, often underlies the noninterference of the hierarchy in the improper care of souls. But, as in cases of war, economic depressions, and disease, the more public authority remains bystanders to emerging reality, the larger the wars, the greater the government restriction of freedom, the more radical the eventual, perhaps hopeless, surgery. If bishops had terminated Charles Curran in

1967 instead of 1986, there might be no need in 1994 of *Ordinances for Catholic Colleges.*

Some bishops beget enemies by being strong voices on behalf of the faith or by inhibiting scandalmongers by the very strength of their policies. There are also prelates, today, who do not think with the Church, certainly not with John Paul II. From Arius and Athanasius onward, the Church has had her share of bad bishops along with the good, true shepherds and deceitful hirelings. Those who break the diocesan bank, or fall into public sin, or otherwise prove incompetent frequently receive a large amount of empathy because they are truly contrite. But haughty collaborators with a watered-down faith or with disobedience resent being watched, let alone being found wanting. Especially by the Pope. Good bishops may be obliged to fight alone against crises which they did not create, waiting for someone — perhaps the Pope, perhaps a consortium of like-minded bishops, perhaps their national conference — to turn the Church around. A succession of Piuses, III, IV, and V, and bishops like Charles Borremeo, Robert Bellarmine, and Stanislaus Hosius did that in the Tridentine period. Not only were they very good at negative defense, but their offensive on behalf of Catholic truth was splendid and victorious.

In recent years, American bishops have dawdled too long at the water's edge of an ecclesiastical Dunkirk. The time has come, with good planning and firm will, for bishops to regroup and to reclaim the Church's own beachheads of evangelization and to resecure in God's good time what should be islands of assent and obedience wherever the name *Catholic* is carved in stone.

Every mortal body, even one whose constitution is hardly biological, must be unified around whatever principle gives it life. Sickness, disease, evil habits are tolerable as long as they are controllable. Once they become prevalent or virulent, dying begins in earnest unless remedied by prayers and persuasion or contained by the good discipline which results from unity among pastors. In many countries still bearing the name Catholic, the Church's faith as an intellectual or moral reality is hardly alive. For a similar tragedy to befall the Church in the United States would be a great failure, considering the confidence placed in American Catholics by a succession of recent vicars of Christ.

EPILOGUE
WHERE IS THE CHURCH GOING?

From Whence She Came

Hopefully, the Church goes from whence she came to where she is supposed to go, presumptively with reasonable effectiveness and with her integrity intact. The gates of hell are not expected to prevail. Still the Church is in the hands of Christians who are also children of their secular cultures and who create difficulty for pastors, as they did for Christ during his public ministry. Indeed, the Mystical Body is a longitudinal macrocosm of the original Passion. Down the centuries among the proclaimed believers have been many who would rather redesign Christ's patrimony than enhance it.

John Tracy Ellis liked to recite a maxim of historians, to wit, that those who do not know or remember history are bound to repeat its mistakes. After two millennia, however, one would think the mistakes would be fewer. After all, history is drama, salvation history mysterious, but in either case the actors are readily identifiable—as heroes or villains. The glory of the Church's existence has been her courageous churchmen, her saints and martyrs, counterbalanced in numbers by her heretics, schismatics, and scoundrels.

The Church always lives in tension with the cultures in which she functions. Christians sometimes choose to judge the Word of God or redefine it, using secular ideologies as the norm. Dissenters, within the ecclesial sanctuary, and public sinners are a fact of

Christian life, but no serious problem to evangelization occurs unless they gain, over a period of time, control of Church offices and infrastructures. What might be called "The Arian Virus" has plagued the Church from the fourth century. Arius, a priest, believing that Christ was not really God's Son ("one in being with the Father") would have been a minor figure in history had not he and his cohorts come to dominate Church bodies, including episcopal sees.

Even after Arius was condemned by the Council of Nicea (325) and exiled, his cause was taken up by a politically astute bishop, Eusebius of Nicomedia (later of Constantinople), who reworded the Nicean formula of Christ's Sonship in such a way that any Christian could sign it, a trick used by dissenters to this day. Using his influence with the Emperor he imposed Arian bishops everywhere in the East. St. Athanasius was exiled more than once for his Nicean faith. Popes of that day also sat somewhat isolated in Peter's Chair, often claiming a debatable primacy. Almost a century later, St. Jerome (327–420) summarized what became in time the schism of the East from Roman Orthodoxy: "The whole world groaned to find itself Arian." Time and time again other alien viruses would sicken the ecclesial body. Whenever Catholic centers of authority fell into the hands of those whose convictions about the Church were ambiguous or hostile to her received message, her nature, or her authority, ecclesial decline set in.

In due course the Church survived Arianism because of outstanding governance in Rome. The only three popes to whom posterity has given the name "the Great"—Leo I (440–61), Gregory I (590–604), and Nicholas I (858–67)—ascended to the Church's Primatial See at providential moments. Recovery can be credited also to great bishops who emerged in the right place at the right time—men like Augustine, Anselm, Cyril, Methodius, and Patrick. The recovery is also due to saintly founders of religious orders whose followers supplied the charisms and the piety needed to complement effective Church administration. St. Basil in the East

(329–79) and St. Benedict in the West (480–560) set the pace for those later monks and religious women who effectively helped popes evangelize Europe.

The thirteenth has been called the greatest of Christian centuries, because papal influence on the countries of Europe had reached its height, especially during the pontificate of Innocent III (1198–1216); and because saintly thinkers like Albert (d. 1280), Thomas Aquinas (d. 1274), and Bonaventure (d. 1274) dominated Catholic intellectual life and its first universities; because Cistercians, Dominicans, Franciscans, and third orders flourished, and because a first rate Fourth Lateran Council (1215) tightened the Church supervision of far-flung dioceses. Ecclesial power brought its inevitable corruption, however: entanglement of Church with affairs of state, royal or otherwise, princely interference in Church administration (the naming of bishops and popes included), worldly and nationalistic prelates becoming an ordinary life experience of the laity, immorality in high and low places, and university personnel from Paris to Prague spinning off anti-Catholic theories about God and the Church. By the fourteenth century—and for forty years, at least—two, at one time three, popes ingloriously reigned, not always in Rome.

Subsequently, and almost as a by-product, groups like the Albigenses, outraged by what they saw, spurned the Church and her sacraments, including marriage, the very basis of any society that called itself Christian. The Albigenses were a particular threat because they organized their own schools, conducted their own workshops, and gained influence with France's ruling elite. Local bishops of the day did not seem to recognize the menace, but Innocent III did. In desperation he organized a crusade to wipe them out. The fourteenth century, a time of profound ecclesial division and decline, set the stage for other heretics like the Conciliarists, and eventually for Martin Luther. The Council of Constance (1414) may have put an end to a three-pope Church, but it also declared a Council superior to a pope. Martin V

(1417–31) and his immediate successors spent their pontificates defending themselves and the Church against priests like John Wycliffe and Jan Hus.

The Protestant rebellion succeeded not simply because princes of the realm lusted to dethrone the popes but because its cause was simply taught within a nationalistic framework and because "the Reformation" (like Albigensianism earlier) assumed command of traditional Catholic institutions. This takeover occurred at the very time Catholic leadership was indecisive, or sought peace through compromise. Luther made his break in 1517 and was excommunicated in 1520; the Council of Trent was finally convoked in 1545, not to complete its mission until 1563. By then England, Northern Germany, all of Scandinavia, and almost all of Poland were lost to the Church. (France in time would become only nominally Catholic.)

If the Church recovered after Luther, Calvin, and Knox, credit must be given, this side of Providence, to a succession of first-rate popes—Paul III (1534–49), Julius III (1550–55), Paul IV (1555–59), Pius IV (1560–65), St. Pius V (1566–72), Gregory XIII (1572–85) and Sixtus V (1585–90). Paul III, who initiated Trent, seemingly stood alone in his will to reform the Church. His initial effort (1538) collapsed because only five bishops showed up. German bishops—who, one would think, were devastated most by Luther's defiance—demonstrated stolid indifference to a Council. Eventually, papal authority controlled the damage and reformed what local churches remained Catholic, as well as the Curia, just about the time explorers were opening new worlds for Catholic missionaries.

Creative legislation, wisely enforced, was only one element in ecclesial reform. Rome positioned a network of reform-minded ecclesiastics, up to and including cardinals (e.g., Charles Borromeo, Stanislaus Hosius), in strategic sees and offices. Monasteries and convents were renewed through the intervention of Theatines, Jesuits, Capuchins, and Ursulines driven by the spiritual programs of saints like Ignatius, preachers like Peter Canisius, and missionaries like Francis Xavier. The particular genius of St. Pius V was his ability to have the decrees of Trent obeyed.

The next deadly threat to the Church came in the eighteenth century, with the so-called French Enlightenment of anti-Catholic, anti-papal elites, and later with a full-blown revolt of the masses against state and Church. The intellectual arguments against revealed religion were easier to combat than the widely publicized mockery and sneering against things religious by literati. The Church was buffetted, too, by the strange appeal of a rigorous Jansenist cult, cultivated by bishops who were more French (Gallican) than Catholic (Roman). When the passion for revolution finally took over the French Assembly, it was voting parish priests who led the way, and bishops like Tallyrand, too. Not only was Church property nationalized, but the clergy became vassals of an anti-Catholic government. In a peculiar way, the further destruction of the Church came to a halt only with Napoleon, who, no great believer himself, decided that Catholic piety was useful to his nefarious purposes.

The "Modernist Crisis" of the nineteenth and twentieth centuries is little more than the maturation of earlier heresies and of the Enlightenment. It was less anti-Catholic perhaps but more anti-Christian, if Christianity means a religion coming from on high and priests deputed to explain it. Catholicity (to the Modernist) was viable if it allowed itself to be reformed along scientific, humanistic, personalist lines. While Modernism might not have been per se a movement or a conspiracy, it was a frame of mind which reduced Catholic faith to a search for the sublimination of humanity, not the worship of a transcendent God. Pius IX, with some help from Leo XIII before he became Pope, and Pius X, closed ranks against it, viewing Modernism as little more than a baptized pagan revolution. (Pius XI and Pius XII would take a similar position, and, prior to Vatican II, many bishops consulted by John XXIII, thought the issue should be revisited.) Unfortunately, defending the Catholic creed in the public forum was made to appear primarily as a defense of monarchy, or of closed societies or mercantilist economics or of clericalism. Propogandists for Enlightenment or Modernism made the case, rather successfully, that the Church was against rational inquiry, personal freedom, political equality, and human betterment in this life. This public relations battle with seculars was lost by the Church. Many of those who filled Catholic teaching chairs began to question the final authority of Catholic hierarchy to determine what Christianity really is.

For the first six decades of the twentieth century, popes and bishops effectively quarantined or contained elites who spoke the Church message falsely or ambiguously or who trivialized faith statements as if they represented the theological view of only one school, or who marginalized Catholic apologists within the Church herself. It seemed as if Arius had finally been buried. Yet as we move to celebrate the thirtieth anniversary of the close of Vatican II (1995) many present-day Catholic apologists think that Arius has risen again. The very forces that the Church historically has used to reform or sanctify herself are now arrayed against any ecclesial governance consistent with the Church's Catholic nature. A "knowledge class"—i.e., organized theologians, canonists, religious educators, the superiors of major religious communities, and the administrators of Catholic educational and welfare institutions, thus far, with the help of well-situated Churchmen—are resisting by force attempts to bring their activity under the definitions and laws of the Church. They also do violence to vulnerable subjects, those who challenge their anti-Roman policies. Rome may issue corrections, but the anti-Church forces which remain are uninhibited by the National Conferences of Bishops or apostolic nuncios, ecclesial officers who normally are the ecclesial channels for effecting assent and obedience within the Church.

The Lesson Unlearned

The evil effects of what can happen to the Church, when long-lived control of Catholic infra-structures fall into the hands of those who do not believe what the Church teaches as true and right, is the particular bequest of Arianism.

The issue is always what it was then, viz., faith, not theology.

The inability or unwillingness of Rome and/or particular hierarchies to deal effectively with ecclesial disorder and declines in Catholic worship is as noticeable today as it was in the fourth century, but today no emperors are around to blame. Still, the positive lesson of history is also clear: Whenever the Church recovers her own dynamism, uses the Catholic apologists at hand to articulate the evils proposed by heretics or schismatics, or to become Catholic counter-revolutionaries, the Church recovers her initiative to conduct evangelization out of her hard-won wisdom. Persuasion is important, but battles with an intransigent enemy are never won by persuasion alone. Arius knew that; so did Martin Luther; so do Charles Curran, Richard McCormick, and Richard McBrien.

The fact that persuasion has not worked to accomplish what Vatican II hoped it would should be clear to everyone by the most casual observation of events since 1965. Those who interpreted the Council's documents as their title to redefine Catholicity, if not Christ and Christianity, have had all the better of the battle with the passing of time. Rome and bishops generally have not persuaded religious superiors, college presidents, or theological societies uniformly to obey Church norms, guidelines, or even her canon law. In their turn, prominent spokesmen of these anti-establishment forces deride John Paul II repeatedly, accusing him of trying to extirpate their views from control of Catholic life and to turn back the clock on their successes. They promise their respective audiences, the public media, that their views of the

Church, priesthood, Catholic moral life, even of Christ will prevail in subsequent pontificates.

The present Pope, with all his faith, piety, and brilliance, has challenged the status quo unsuccessfully because officers of *magisterium,* neglecting advice given by St. Paul (1 Tim 1:9), have not with proper results countered the organized force used by rebellious priests and religious to gain control of our institutions. The substantial failure of dissidents to convert *magisterium* to *their* cause is also obvious.

Remaining to be answered are these questions: How long will this stand-off continue? And to whose advantage? Christ faced such questions boldly, reducing the answers to faith or its lack (Jn 10:22ff.).

Clearly, after Vatican II, the worst features of the Arian patrimony became policy in the administration of the American church— difficult teachings of Vatican II muted, division between Rome and national hierarchies, toleration of evasions, misbehavior by clerics and religious, favor shown to anti-magisterial leaders, isolation of Catholic apologists, liberation of Catholic institutions, notably religious orders, from obedience to canon law, preaching but little enforcement of some of the best restatements in history of Catholic teaching and practice. Arius would have been pleased.

Making Disciples in Our Day

Our critical difficulty is not that people continue to be Catholic in name only, nor is it that the young attend Mass or confess their sins with little regularity. What worries many is the nature of the Catholic family in the next century and the nature of those institutions, including the priesthood, religious life, and the parish, on which Christ and families depend for faith and piety.

During crises of any kind, denial is the order of the day, e.g., denial that there has been an erosion of the Catholic faith, that it is

serious, that it is anyone's fault in particular, that it can be remedied on *magisterial* terms. But where there is life—and real Catholic life exists in surprising places—recovery always follows the
application of proper remedies. Chief among these is the unity of
pastors around the Church's received message and ability of these
pastors to incarnate this within their own sacred precincts, even if
it involves dying on their part.

Contemporary pastors make a major mistake by seeming to act
as if the future of Catholicity depends on the peaceful coexistence
with forces of the French Enlightenment, even within their own
house. And with the philosophies which underpin the *modus
operandi* of Modernity. The Catholic Church is a great accom-
modater when she retains her own unity and identity, based on her
own teaching, which she strongly supports within her household.
Teaching without internal institutional support is always vain
teaching. If the renewal promised by John XXIII has failed, it is for
the reason that important Church institutions have allowed themselves, or have been allowed, to separate themselves from the vicar
of Christ. Party to that separation have been blocs of bishops whose
policies after Vatican II reflected more the thinking of Rudolf
Bultmann, Martin Heidegger, Max Weber, or Carl Rogers than
the wisdom contained in Matthew, Mark, Luke, and John, along
with a variety of Pauls and Piuses down through the centuries.

Important ways for sustaining support for things Catholic
involve presenting unashamedly a well-argued case for the truths
which came from the Christian tradition, confronting and correcting
error in timely fashion as needed, and showing favor to those who
are faithful to Catholic teaching. The conversion of those who are
not faithful should be diligently sought, but those who contuma-
ciously insist on subverting the Church should be resisted and,
where necessary, limited in their ability to engage in malfeasance
of office.

One of the least-reported scandals of the post-Vatican II Church
is the extent of suffering, after 1965, among those Catholics whose

offense seems only to have been that they accepted the Church at her word about what was legitimate renewal, as distinct from false teaching and bad example. To their surprise, they discovered that those who did not take the Church at her word, or had doubts about it, had taken over the best seats at the ecclesial table. These newcomers to status and power, with hardly any sustained resistance, appeared to be the voice of Vatican II progress, while ordinary churchgoers were said to represent the disavowed past. Defense of the faith was not totally out of style, of course, as long as its spokesmen were prepared to accept new meaning for the old words Church authority still insisted on using.

This reversal of good order may have done great damage to the faithful but even more so to their children and to the Church's public image. Now that these scandals must be repaired, wisdom and courage of a special quality will be needed by those charged with the responsibility to restore all things in Christ. Unquestionably, evildoers will be outraged because their sowing of revolutionary cockle in the Church's fields has been terminated somewhat before eternity. Christ did counsel patience with individual evildoers, but he was himself outraged by hypocritical institutional leaders who defiled the faith and holiness of his little ones. Better for them to lose a job, or status, or income, or tenure, or preferment than to enter eternity as willful scandalmongers, subject to Christ's doleful judgment. And the same holds true for compatriots or superiors who collaborate, actively or if only by silence, in the continued defilement of his Mystical Body. It will not be easy this time to sift the chaff from the wheat, because the newer breed of disrupter is unlikely to say what Charles Curran said more than once: The Church is wrong. Later dissenters are more likely to hide behind a misunderstood context or nuance or, when challenged, say, "I no longer hold that." However reform occurs, one rule of thumb makes sense: Only men and women of strong, enthusiastic, and demonstrated faith ought to be in charge of our Catholic institutions.

Over fifty years ago a pastor could walk into a parochial school, a bishop or provincial into a religious house, an apostolic delegate into a diocese, and freely ask questions of anyone he chose about how well or poorly things were going. Most of those visits were scheduled regularly, although sometimes they came as a response to frequent complaints. At the turn of the twentieth century, it was not uncommon for a bishop on an "episcopal visitation" to stay overnight in a parish, available to anyone in the parish who wished to speak to him during the allotted time span. Usually, he was not looking for trouble, but neither was he unwilling to face it should he find it. Respect for his office and the role he played was commonplace. If such visitations continued to occur even after they became dead letters, they happened nonetheless and were accepted as proper. The principle of good government was sound, even if its application was less than perfect.

In those days, should trouble occur, the heavy hand of authority might fall occasionally, if wrongly, on some poor unfortunate who was more feisty or fallible than evildoer. But the system saw to it that real troublemaking teachers, principals, and parish priests were properly corrected or transferred. If performance is the gauge, the system worked the way it was intended to work. And if we had become neglectful in supervision by the time of World War II, the oversight of earlier superiors still reaped its harvest. In 1971, when so many dioceses were suffering through serious upheavals, I found the Archdiocese of Philadelphia to be a model of serenity and good Catholic behavior. Speaking with a group of pastors one night, I asked an innocent outsider's question: "Is this because of Cardinal Krol?" One pastor shot back immediately: "No, because of Cardinal Dougherty!" Dougherty had been dead twenty years by then.

Today, it need not be said that any of those religious authorities walking into a self-styled Catholic institution without notice, or permission, may sense he is not welcome, be told there is nothing to discuss, or be told off. And effectively denied the right of oversight, especially if it might end up in criticism of a status quo, even of a status quo causing scandal. Interlocutory discourse, sometimes called dialogue, especially between superiors and their subjects, may beget pleasantries and, for that reason if for no other, be all that one can say about the ongoing relationship. But it is not oversight. And in the end, lack of oversight begets lack of discipline, and of unity, for which Church authorities alone are responsible. A Church in which the right of oversight is denied to legitimate and approved pastors, one way or another, is Catholic in name only. And the only way to restore oversight to its proper place in the Church is to do it.

We are dealing here with evil. The failure to see that the catechism of the catholic church is taught effectively everywhere, as the Baltimore Catechism once was, will be a greater evil, indeed. The Church has a great deal to say these days about evils in the world but is not attending effectively to the evils going on within herself. Christ also said a good deal on this subject. Once, in a special way to his disciple Nicodemus, who found it easier to confess his faith in the darkness of the night, the Lord specified the Christian priority:

> God did not send the Son into the world
> to condemn the world,
> but that the world might be saved through him.
> Whoever believes in him avoids condemnation,
> but whoever does not believe is already condemned
> for not believing in the name of God's only Son.
> The judgment is this:
> the light came into the world,
> but men loved darkness rather than light
> because their deeds are wicked.
> Everyone who practices evil
> hates the light;

he does not come near it
for fear his deeds will be exposed.
But he who acts in truth
comes into the light,
to make clear
that his deeds are done in God (Jn 3:17–21).

Relearning St. Athanasius

The rise and fall of any institution is related to the ability of its
leadership to sustain reasonable regard and enthusiasm for its
reason for existence and for the way of life it proposes. Behavior
in the ranks may not always coincide uniformly with "the tradition"
or with "the law of the land" or with "the gospel". Still, in vital
communities large portions of membership do, and a majority at
least know and respect the institution itself. If the community is
very good, pride of membership is part of this picture, and a
certain joy in leadership, too. This is true even when the best and
the brightest sometimes bend the rules while leaving the system
intact. If the corporate body functions as it should, anyone can
manage it. Institutions do not survive their third or fourth
generation, however, when their leadership is consistently pedes-
trian and when charismatic characters, with the capacity to regen-
erate tired systems according to norm, are lacking.

Charismatics create institutions which grow to be managed by
bureaucratic types. Charismatics are like architects, men of ideas.
Bureaucrats are engineers or mechanics, who, when they are
good, know where to place the nuts and bolts which give stability
to the structure and its operation. Charismatics create the cause,
assemble and inspire the disciples; good administrators foster rou-
tine development and order, and also protect the structures necessary for the preservation of their founders' vision. Idea men with
dynamic personalities and rhetorical ability gained the attention

of their followers originally because they have a credible message which they motivate people to accept. After they are gone, longevity depends on good managers.

Ralph Waldo Emerson once called an institution the lengthened shadow of a man. Group or corporate life represents and replaces the person of the founder. The world gained a Christian Church once disciples were chosen to protect and govern the common good of the faithful according to norms which Christ proclaimed as gospel.

Effective successors to the apostle role had three qualities: (1) firm convictions themselves about the wisdom of the original charter and unqualified dedication to its preservation and propagation; (2) the ability to preach the message effectively and to assemble faithful disciples in an institutional framework; and (3) skill at governing diverse populations and interest groups, frequently in conflict with each other over the group's nature and mission. The talent of good government went beyond the "Bully Pulpit" concept. Favor was bestowed upon the faithful disciples, while restraint within reason, by internal controls or public law, contained those disruptive or evil forces which inevitably arose. Christ himself made a distinction between "the good shepherd" and "the hireling", and appealed to good governance in accordance with his image of the sheepfold. Charismatics sometimes lack the ability to govern wisely what they or someone else has created. Those who inherit the mantle of authority may govern in times of peace or during crisis. Different qualities are required in each situation. Crisis management, especially when the anti-institutional force within is motivated by ill-will toward authority or hatred, or led by charismatics or by opinion-molders skilled in power politics, calls for extraordinary talent at governing, and remarkable courage besides. Those who handle prosperity effortlessly are often the least qualified to handle upheaval, just as revolutionaries rarely are competent to deliver what they promise.

It may not be out of place to consider that what is going on within the Church today is to moderns as "seductive" (St. Augustine's term) as Arianism was at the time of St. Athanasius. The Church in Africa in the fourth century was as important to Christendom as the Church of the United States is to contemporary Catholicity. Athanasius and the popes of his day often stood as minority figures against a majority of their neighboring peers in their efforts to protect the integrity of early Christianity. Athanasius and the popes did not stem leakage from the Church by themselves because other saints, scholars, and monks came to the Church's rescue. But the Bishop of Alexandria, better than most, did recognize threatening doctrinal issues then, as clearly as Paul VI and John Paul II understand the basis of our modern Catholic crisis.

Said he at the time:

> It will not be out of place to consider the ancient tradition, teaching and faith of the Catholic Church, which was revealed by the Lord, proclaimed by the Apostles, and guarded by the Fathers. For upon this faith the Church is built, and if anyone were to lapse from it he would no longer be Christian either in fact or in name (Letter to Serapion).

INDEX

Academic freedom, 100

Academics, 34, 56

Albigenses, 133–34

Alexander VI, 28–29

Ambiguity, doctrinal, 100

American Catholic Experience,
11

American Catholic People, 11

*American Catholics and intellec-
tual life,* 49

Americanism, 38

antimagisterial forces, 71–73,
75

Apostolic times, 28

Arand, S.S., Fr. Louis, 48

Archbishop, 62

Archbishops, role of, 93

Arian Virus, 132, 137, 138

Arius, 100, 136

Association of Catholic Colleges and Universities,
113, 115

Authority, Church (*Magisterium*), 7, 10, 12, 15, 17, 48,
58–59

Autonomy, 39, 42, 69, 73

Avignon captivity, 42

Balthasar, Fr. Hans Urs von,
35

Baltimore Catechism, 15, 37

Baltimore, Third Council of,
36–39

Battle for the American Church,
7, 9–10, 21, 34, 71ff, 76

Becker, S.J., Fr. Joseph, 49

"Belgian Block", the, 42

Beltran, Bishop Eusebius J.,
82

Benestad, J. Brian, 80

Berger, Peter, 104

Bernardin, Joseph Cardinal,
69, 76–77, 81–82

Bernanos, Georges, 25

Berrigan, Daniel, 80

Berrigan, Philip, 19

Birth Control Commission,
20, 66

Bishop Eusebius of
Nicomedia, 132

Bishops, 11–12, 24, 32, 39–40,
46–48, 49ff, 61ff, 73, 81,
91ff, 101

Bishops' responsibility, 91ff.

Bismarck, Otto von, 17

Bouyer, Fr. Louis, 10

Brown, S.S., Fr. Raymond,
50ff, 74, 79, 86
  "Detective Work", 52

Brownson, Orestes, 39